MY BELOVED WILDERNESS

Also by Phil Drabble

BADGERS AT MY WINDOW

Frontispiece Author in his study at Goat Lodge

MY BELOVED WILDERNESS

Phil Drabble

Illustrations by S. C. Porter

PELHAM BOOKS

First published in Great Britain by
MICHAEL JOSEPH LTD
52 Bedford Square
London W.C.1
1971

7207 0519 3

Printed in Great Britain by Northumberland Press Limited, Gateshead, in eleven on twelve point Baskerville on paper supplied by P. F. Bingham Ltd., Croydon, Surrey, and bound by Dorstel Press, Harlow.

To all who prefer a full life in quiet places to glittering insecurity studded with status symbols.

Contents

Illustrations

Preface

Having spent half a lifetime working five days a week to pay for my pleasures in the remaining two, I am in a fair position to compare my present lot with the factory life I knew.

I get no more expense account meals, no company car nor free travel abroad. If the ink in my pen runs dry I could be as cold as the charity of a takeover bid.

On the credit side, I live far from crowds among the animals and birds I love. My dogs are my constant companions and I have no fear of them climbing on my back for promotion.

I come and go as I please, with birdsong instead of a factory buzzer to wake me out of sleep and my surroundings are so steeped in history that I should be dull indeed if I was oblivious to its atmosphere.

Instead of going to visit lovely places or on expeditions to watch rare birds or interesting animals, I live among them close enough to know them personally. My life may be simple but it is beyond price.

CHAPTER ONE

The cage

Long before I had sweated away twenty odd years in Industry, I came to the conclusion that five days working with folk I often disliked, for bosses I rarely respected, was a prohibitive price to pay for the pleasure of two days rural solitude at the tag end of the week.

The simplest country cottage held more seduction for me than the flashiest house in a stockbroker belt, where first prize in the rat race was to cram the drive with 'Jags' and boats and caravans.

I decided it would be more sensible to settle for less money with more freedom, but I knew that the glamour of the most folksy olde worlde cottage would soon wear thin without the brass to keep it up.

It was easy enough to pipe dream a theory that simple things have deepest values because I preferred the logic of slow rural minds to the sharp wits of the smoothest city slickers.

Factory life had often meant no more to me than cudgelling my brains in witch hunts for economies that merely masked redundancies. It was mental prostitution compared to creative work which would leave the world a better place.

I pined to spend my life with country folk in a job where time had no importance. I longed for dewy dawns and starlit nights, birdsong in spring and the white solitudes of winter.

I wanted to be an independent individual instead of a tooth in a cog in an industrial wheel. I itched for the luxury of cocking a snook at anyone who happened to annoy me and of opting out of the internal politics which beslime most large concerns.

It was easy enough to define what I wanted but it needed courage to grasp the nettle to get it. Such starry-eyed ambitions rarely bring the bacon home.

I have since discovered what good company I was in. Now that I live in deep country with wild deer across the paddock and the song of woodland birds to prise me out of sleep at dawn, my friends all say how lucky I am.

When they see that I have escaped from the cage they tell me how marvellous it must be to work for myself and I am bound to admit that I have never slaved for a master half so good!

I come when I like and go as I please, work among wild creatures in peaceful places and meet a succession of people with interests in common.

My dogs are my constant companions and there is scarcely a soul on earth I would rather be with. Friends say that they long to retire so that they, too, can idle away their time as I do. They do not realise that earning a living with one's pen is harder than it seems.

They envy me my complexion, forgetting that the colour in my cheeks often owes more to harsh winds and stinging rain than to soft sunlight. They have never tried carrying buckets of water to livestock when the handle sticks to their flesh with frost, or waited motionless to watch some woodland rarity while gnats and mosquitoes devour them alive.

They have no conception of gales so cold that their guts would turn to water nor the backaching agony of cleaning out a ditch or tramping all day in muddy wellingtons.

Most of them delude themselves that life in the country

is an idyllic mush of dainty daffodils and birds which sing a sickly song of praise instead of hissing hate at rivals who dare dispute their territory.

I looked these snags in the eye before I burned my boats, so that most of my surprises have been pleasant ones.

My overwhelming yearning for country things owes nothing to environment. I was born in an industrial town in Staffordshire's Black Country, where the first sound at dawn was a tramcar clattering past the bedroom window at four o'clock in the morning.

We had no garden but a grey-flagged yard so shaded by the next house that even ivy wouldn't grow. The wildest birds which visited us were house sparrows as grey with grime as the rain which industrial smog thickened into soup.

The man next door was a coal merchant who kept a few carthorses in the stable and a dog in the yard. The poor creature barked incessantly except for brief respites when the groom who supervised the stables thrashed him into silence. Continuous solitary confinement had made him so savage that I was forbidden for my own safety to touch or comfort him, as I so longed to do.

There was a hunter in the loose box next to the carthorses, for our neighbour was keen on his sport if unimaginative about his dog; so my first childhood memories of animals were the lovely smell of stabled horses and the miseries of a dog sobbing for affection and companionship and freedom.

Although traffic roared past the front door, there were fields at the back of the house. Not fields as lush green as country fields, because my father was a doctor with an industrial practice and had to live on the job.

In those days the land was what its name implied and the wiry grass at the back of our house flaunted russet autumnal tints even in high summer.

It was the only grass I knew, and it cloaked the foothills of grey mounds of ragged cinder. Strangers saw these spoil-banks from coal pits and iron works as the dereliction of previous prosperity; to me they were exciting mountains to be scaled.

Most thrilling of all were the rushy black pools left as a memorial when the fertile land gave up the fight and sank below the water surface due to mining subsidence.

'Swags,' we called them because the earth's flaccid crust had sagged—or 'swagged'—when the coal had been torn out far below. They were ideal for a child to explore because the edges were usually shallow gentle slopes, so that stupidity was unlikely to be punished by worse than a wetting.

There was plenty of weed in them growing food for water beetles and sticklebacks, leeches and fiery-bellied newts.

I am an only child and grew up immune from the itch to herd in gangs. I was always happy on my own, poking about with a fishing net on the edge of one of these swags or quietly searching hedges or weedy patches for caterpillars, with the dedicated patience of a monkey catching fleas.

There were always rows of jamjars on our window sills, with newts and water scorpions, snails and whirligig beetles and water boatmen.

Neither of my parents knew or cared about natural history, so my early mistakes nearly all spelled tragedy. I didn't realise that fish took oxygen from the water and was surprised to find my sticklebacks stiff and dead next day. Knowing nothing about the dangers of overcrowding, I simply thought I hadn't given them enough food. So I aggravated their complaint by filling the jars with all sorts of goodies, which depleted the oxygen in the water even more rapidly than the fish.

Nobody told me that newts hibernated, so I kept mine in jamjars of water all winter till the dreadful day when a hard frost embalmed them in solid ice like trout in aspic.

The more vividly I recall those childhood days, the worse seem the atrocities I perpetrated in blind ignorance.

The one advantage about being reared in the Black Country was that, however industrialised it had become, most of the inhabitants were removed from real country ancestors by no more than one or two generations.

Their grandfathers or great grandfathers probably migrated from Wales or the heart of rural Shropshire during the Industrial Revolution and a nostalgic love of country things still ran through their souls.

Local boys of my generation were inveterate bird nesters and hunters of butterflies and pickers of wild flowers. They were often deliberately cruel, though more from lack of imagination than from the virulence of vandals.

Their parents kept fighting cocks and Stafford bull terriers, which they matched in the dog pit. If we persuaded a great autumn orb spider to spin her web in a jam jar, and introduced a wasp to do battle with her, it was mild amusement by comparison.

We sat there entranced, laying bets in marbles or sweets, backing the spider to enmesh the wasp before it stung her to death or staking our fortunes that the wasp would emerge buzzing hate but undefeated.

If the spider triumphed, she became a 'oner' as in conkers, and I recall the proud moment when my favourite warrior reached double figures in her victims. I crowned her a 'tenner' and released her to honourable retirement, to procreate her pedigree kind as stock for next season.

That was typical of the Black Country of those days. Countrymen and their descendants who lived there treasured their inherited arts of stockmanship. Their grandfathers had probably grown great bullocks weighing a ton and had hung sides of bacon from twenty score pigs on their walls instead of pictures.

The woman who kept the shop at the corner of our street was a patient of my father's and always kept two pigs in her sty, one for herself and the other for us. I used to go down once a week, to see how it was coming on and to watch her grooming it with a dandy brush as carefully as if it was a racehorse. Yet when the time came to kill it, she turned out with the rest to watch the 'sticking' as avidly as the Romans watched the sports in their arena.

These folk practised their stockman's art with roller canaries and racing pigeons, whippets and fighting cocks. The skills of their forebears blossomed with their prize-winning chrysanthemums and gaudy carnations. No farmer cajoled more from his land than they did from their allotments which produced two-pound onions and four-foot leeks.

Small wonder that their sons knew by instinct that fish did better in enamel buckets with plenty of water than in fancy goldfish bowls which let light in all round. They needed no telling that caterpillars going off their grub were more likely getting ready to pupate than suffering from constipation.

They put garden riddles over nests of fledglings so that their parents fed them to maturity, then had no compunction about putting them in cages just when they were ready to fly away. They even blinded them with red hot needles so that they spent their lives in song because they were oblivious of the fact that the horizon was limited by the far side of the street.

The extraordinary thing is that none of this struck me as being particularly cruel. I took it all so much for granted that I was only interested in the skills of bird fanciers who could catch goldfinches on thistles with bird lime or snare hawfinches in thickets with a horsehair noose. The miseries of wild things sentenced for life to the proximity of Man never so much as crossed my mind.

As I grew older I graduated to more exciting things. I struck up a friendship with Hairy Kelly the local professional rat catcher.

He was no cossetted bureaucrat who could get away with no more knowledge than is necessary to put a spoonful of poison down a rathole and fill up a form about it in triplicate. Hairy believed in private enterprise. He was self-employed and if he didn't run his business at a profit, he didn't eat. Far worse, he didn't drink.

I never knew Hairy go short of a drink, which is some yardstick not only of his skill but of the native wit which motivated him. If he couldn't prove he'd caught a rat, he wasn't paid. It was as simple as that. So he kept all his captures as visual evidence and charged his clients in direct proportion to the number of rats he produced.

This figure was sometimes subject to a certain amount of manipulation. Nobody ever thought of searching his person when he arrived. He was a lone bachelor who, if my nose was to be relied on, subsisted mainly on a diet of stale beer and stale haddock. Sensitive people approached no closer than was strictly necessary.

Those who suspected that all the rats claimed as victims had not been caught that day were wiser to keep such opinions to themselves, since Hairy was a tetchy man, quite liable to tip out a whole sackful of live rats in a client's house if he thought he'd been affronted. He would then refuse to have anything further to do with them.

I never got involved in the commercial aspects of Hairy's work apart from buying an occasional ferret from him. My delight was to go out ratting and learning to 'work' the ferrets in ricks and hedgerows and under fowlpen floors, and I must have been useful because he even let me take Mick, my old half-bred bull terrier. When Mick's vice-like jaws had embraced a rat it was no good to sell alive for training someone's pup.

I imagine, too, that I lent a slightly spurious air of respectability to the outfit so that he could wheedle invitations where he would otherwise have been unwelcome.

In return, he taught me some of the tricks of his trade. A tiny cobweb across the mouth of a hole meant that there was nothing at home and it would be a waste of time to try the ferret. I learned that rats will not bolt clean unless they think they know a better hole to go to.

Hairy always 'worked' them towards a stream or rick or drain where they thought they would be safe. At the last moment he cut off their retreat with a net from which he took them as easily as balls from the pocket of a billiards table.

If he had tried to bolt them from good cover into the open they would have preferred to stay underground and fight the ferret.

This taught me the basic principles of wildlife management which have proved invaluable since, but he also taught me a lot about human nature too. Men are as much the slaves of habit as animals are. I learned that if we were prepared to continue ratting into the dinner hour on a farm, all the hangers-on and other uninvited guests disappeared as if by magic.

It was then often possible, by moving up the hedge a little, to switch quarry from rats to rabbits and to 'nab a few long eared 'uns instead of all long tailed 'uns', as Hairy put it. These were hidden in a convenient ditch and collected on the way home.

Hairy taught me to snare rabbits and foxes and to catch rats and stoats in deadfall traps and gins. And I soon learned that 'once a client, always a client'. He kept a few virile rats to restock profitable premises he had cleared too thoroughly.

While Hairy caught the odd rabbit as a sideline, Jago thought of nothing else. Jago was the local policeman and everybody knew him as Bobby Jago except his superiors who referred to him patronisingly as Constable Smith. But he was Jago to me and I coveted his whippet more than the most beautiful women in a sultan's harem.

She was a very good whippet, almost twice the size of modern weaklings which mince about at dog-shows or shiver on some silken cushion. She was a working bitch with enough hair in her coat to keep her warm without a whippet rug. I imagine that one of her female ancestors had been frightened by a Bedlington terrier with crocodile jaws.

Although it takes a very good dog to catch a rabbit fair on its own run, any creature of intelligence is bound to grow cunning with as much practice as that bitch had.

She would crouch four or five yards from the rabbit warren, ears pricked and bulging eyes staring, waiting for Jago to creep up and pop a ferret in a hole on the far side of the warren.

Complete silence was the secret of her success and she would sit quivering with expectancy. The first hint of action was the twitch of the whippet's ears as she caught the rumbling of movement underground. Her muscles tautened and she would slide a yard or so this way or that anticipating the exact hole from which the rabbit would bolt, as a scrum-half waits for the ball to break from the scrum.

Nine times out of ten the bitch was right. Nine times out of ten she 'happened' to be slap in the path the rabbit chose and one crack of her crocodile jaws was all that it needed.

Jago and I loved the tenth time best. Then the rabbit

would come out the wrong side of the hedge or two rabbits would bolt at once and one would get clean away.

Clean away is an exaggeration but it would get far enough to steal twenty yards start before the whippet was after it. I never saw such graceful speed. That dog was craftsman-built as a running machine. Her back arched and flexed as if powered by springs of truest steel, but she didn't always win. There would have been no sport without an element of luck.

But skill often did triumph so that, within a hundred yards or so, she picked her rabbit up and brought it back with pride to settle down and listen for the next eruption.

By rural standards we lived in a slum but the affinity of those Black Countrymen with whom I was brought up infected me incurably. They sowed the seeds which grew and flourished so that it became inevitable that I should eventually escape to deep countryside where my spirit already belonged.

This hadn't dawned on me then for I no more dreamed it was possible for me to escape than for a lark from its cage.

I still had to go through school and I hated that. I was forever getting into trouble because I was agin the government and such a rebel. The only distinction I got was to become secretary of the Natural History Society and even that was not because I wanted to learn about wildlife. My poacher friends had forgotten more about practical natural history learned from fieldcraft than my academic school master would ever know.

I had joined to escape organised games and for the chance of sneaking into the woods for a quiet smoke and to poach the odd waterhen, which I roasted in a biscuit tin over a primus stove when I got back to my study.

The fringe benefit was that I got a mild dose of collector's mania and built up a fair collection of butterflies and birds' eggs. Both would be frowned on today, of course, but I often think that the reason many folk are so jealous of their heritage of country things is that they started by collecting them.

By the time I was nineteen I was less interested in wild-life than racing motorbikes and the only birds I liked had feathers in their hats.

My education had taught me to be polite to ladies and call my elders sir, but it had not equipped me to choose a career. There was no way of knowing what any job entailed without taking the irrevocable step of getting involved. By that time it was too late to opt out again if the horizon of the promised land turned out to be a mirage.

In any case the 1930s were so short of opportunities that security counted higher than either compatibility or reward. Anyone who had chosen a job because it offered creative satisfaction or might make the world a better place was rated an impractical idealist and deserved no better than he got.

I was never in much danger of being accused of being starry-eyed. My father had expected me to go into the family practice but I disliked humanity *en masse* when it was well and thought even less of it when it whimpered in complaint. In any case I never worked hard enough to pass the medical exams at Oxford so went to London to read engineering.

The result was that I chose a career for the worst possible reason. I took up engineering, not as a dedicated vocation, but to learn to tune an engine whose thunderous voice had seduced me until its yowling note screamed in an ecstacy of racing pitch.

This blunder cost me a life sentence of twenty-five years in jobs I never liked.

The first month on a factory floor wore the gilt off my

gingerbread. I discovered that the charms of my new mistress had faded before the sun was up and the factory buzzer blew me to my bench at eight o'clock on bitter winter mornings.

The disillusion was even more bitter because I had to travel the six miles to Bilston on a bicycle powered not by a racing engine but by my aching legs. A narrow-minded beak had suspended my driving licence for speeding down Battersea High Street in my last term at London University. My father was disappointed that I had no interest in medicine and threw me in at the deep end of the factory line to sink or swim as best I could. When I came down from University I started at shop floor level in a factory at Bilston. I inhaled the stench of hot whale oil in the toolroom hardening shop and suffered the boredom of minding a machine which did nothing for hours but shave slivers off blanks of soulless steel.

My foreman was a martinet with absolute power to hire and fire and the only thing he wanted to know when I arrived was 'Can you file, son?'

I said I thought I could so he sent me to stores for a piece of steel nine inches long and one inch round. 'We'll see,' he said. 'File that till its three quarters of an inch square.'

He chucked my first three trials on the scrap heap because they were inaccurate. By that time I had leaned over my bench for eight hours a day for three days and had blisters on my palms which felt solid pus to the back of my hands.

To my delight he accepted the fourth attempt and I wondered what it was to be used for. 'Not bad,' he said. 'Now file the corners off till it's three quarters round.'

Two more tries were wasted effort and he obviously thought he'd break my heart so that I'd cause no trouble in the future. At last he accepted one. 'Not bad,' he said.

'You can file now.' And he threw it on the scrap heap.

If it taught me nothing else it taught me what a fool I'd been to choose a job where I worked for somebody else, but the discovery was too late and there was nothing I could do about it.

After that I was upgraded to a milling machine next to Josh the shop steward. Josh and I got on fine. For different reasons we were both prepared to work very hard to outwit authority.

He taught me all the fiddles. We had to clock on and off each job but by starting the next one before we'd clocked off the last, we accumulated enough completed job cards by Saturday morning to do no work at all. We simply handed in completed cards at the appropriate intervals and spent the rest of the time running profitable raffles for packets of cigarettes.

I learned the intricacies of the shop floor grapevine which is so much more effective than any bush telegraph thumped out by uneducated savages. It warns of the approach of Authority and taught me how to fool time study engineers into allowing longer for jobs than I needed.

Within eighteen months I was an accomplished barrack-room lawyer and was looking for a job which would pay more than the miserable 45*s*. a week I was getting there.

Josh said he was glad he wasn't coming with me because I was obviously equipped to become a management scab and would probably degenerate into an even worse bastard than the foreman I disliked so much.

I said I hoped I should and thanked him for teaching me so much of his seditious trade. I would be on my guard for the obstructive likes of him in future.

Management jobs proved hard to come by, so I forsook the conventional approach through personnel offices and started at the top of the tree instead. Hearing that a friend was leaving a firm in West Bromwich, I called at the office next day and asked to see the managing director.

A pale man in a grubby raincoat came into the room and asked what I wanted. Thinking he was the foreman, I repeated my request. He said he was the managing director, so what did I want?

'I've come for the vacant job as assistant to the Works Engineer.' This cut no ice for he said that the job wasn't advertised, he didn't know if they were going to fill it again but he would get in touch with me if he decided that I was the chap for the job. If I had heard nothing in six weeks I could try again.

Six weeks later I demanded to see the managing director once more. The girl at the reception desk, who appeared to combine the job with typing, telephonist and probably making the office tea, was not so forthcoming this time. She didn't believe me when I said I had an appointment and only passed on my message with reluctance.

The boss had obviously forgotten all about me, so I reminded him he had invited me to call in six weeks if I had heard no more and repeated my request.

What appeared to floor him was my reply to his question of what wage I expected. I told him that I would come for nothing for a month and that he could then pay me what I was worth in retrospect.

If it wasn't a better approach than he was used to, it was so different that he obviously couldn't think of an answer so he hired me on trial at £3 a week. I was there for the next twenty-three years and finished on the Board of Directors.

This was no scintillating success story, no saga of the local boy made good. It was a family concern and I had the advantage of being the only member of top management who could talk the same language as the men on the shop floor.

Josh the shop steward and scores of roisterous nights in tough Black Country pubs had taught me things concealed from bosses' sons who try to learn their trade by a few weeks in Father's workshop. Only fools and sychophants would part with secrets to those who might use them later as rods to beat the backs of their mates and themselves.

I knew about factory bookies and mixing daywork with piecework to fiddle time sheets. I knew when kindness was mistaken for softness and when a firm stand would be respected or taken as harshness and only result in more stubborn resistance.

The snag was that I knew the men I controlled so well that I often respected them more than my employers. My loyalties were often so divided that it went against the grain to screw them down in the cause of easy profit and I yearned for my freedom even more.

Dissatisfaction with one's job is common enough, and there were doubtless thousands like me who ached to step off the treadmill, to get away from it all and to escape from the rat race.

The number of such clichés to describe the complaint is symptomatic of its epidemic proportions.

Grumbling about such frustrations did not help. In 1941 I sent my first article to *The Field* more as a protest than in any hope of having it published. Although it was rejected, it was returned with an encouraging letter from Brian Vesey-FitzGerald, who was then editor, inviting me to try again on some subject which I knew more about than anyone else!

It was a tall order but, in this age of specialisation, there is obviously less competition among those who know the last word about the articulation of gnat's knees than among authorities on the internal combustion engine. The only things I could claim to know more about than other literate people were cockfighting and dog fighting.

Some of my friends in Black Country pubs were authorities on both, but putting X for their mark in the columns of football pool coupons was about the pinnacle of their literary ambitions. There was no need to fear their competition in *The Field*.

So I submitted an article on Stafford Bull Terriers and was not only paid for it but invited to do two follow-up pieces about cockfighting. I often wrote for *The Field* after that and built up a connection in radio and television and writing books until, in 1961, I left industry and took the risk of setting out to earn a living with my pen.

It was a formidable decision to take because I was putting not only my future at stake but that of my wife Jess as well. Luckily for me she dislikes towns as much as I do and has little in common with the status symbol conscious folk who would pawn their souls to live like the pseudo élite.

We decided that a simpler life in a more secluded if less fashionable spot was worth the risk involved. A little judgement and a lot of luck had set me free at last.

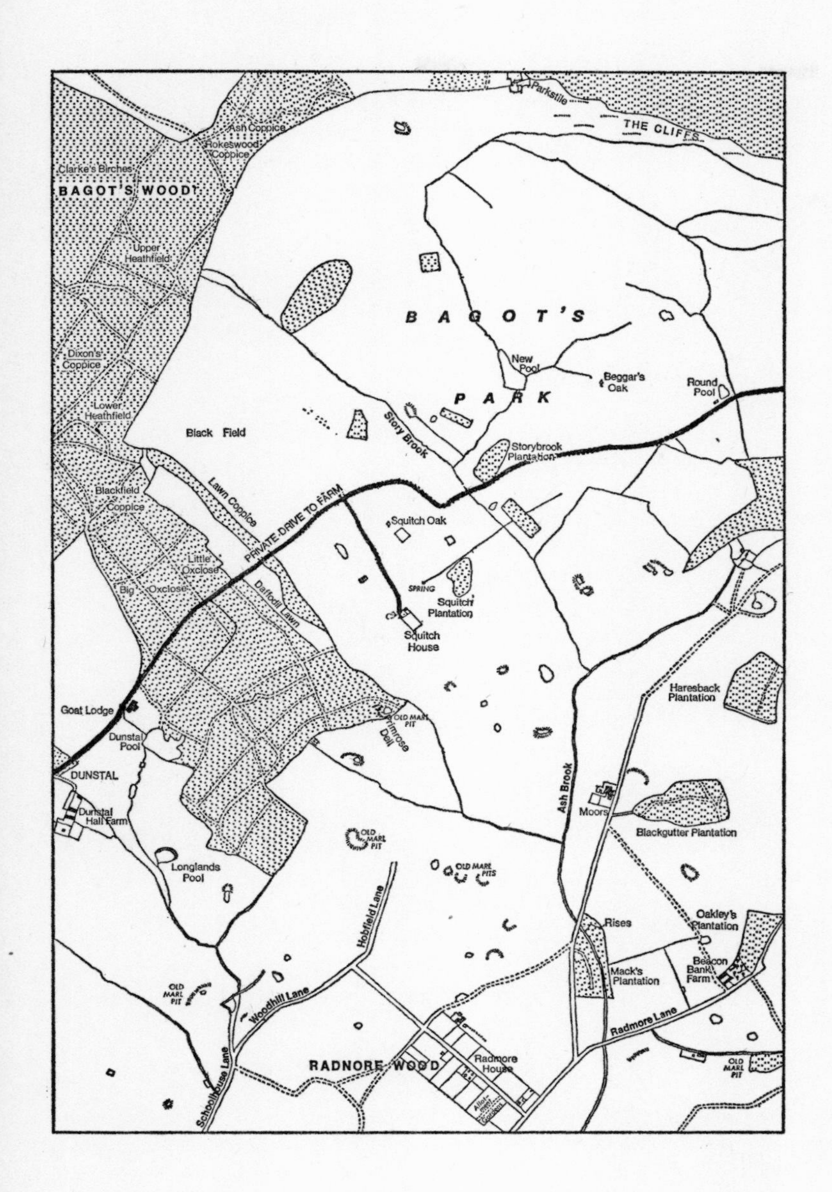
Parkstile
THE CLIFFS
Ash Coppice
Rokeswood Coppice
Clarke's Birches
BAGOT'S WOOD
Upper Heathfield
BAGOT'S PARK
New Pool
Beggar's Oak
Round Pool
Dixon's Coppice
Lower Heathfield
Black Field
Story Brook
Storybrook Plantation
Lawn Coppice
PRIVATE DRIVE TO FARM
Blackfield Coppice
Squitch Oak
Little Oxclose
Big Oxclose
Daffodil Lawn
SPRING
Squitch Plantation
Squitch House
Haresback Plantation
Goat Lodge
OLD MARL PIT
Primrose Dell
Dunstal Pool
DUNSTAL
Ash Brook
Moors
Dunstal Hall Farm
Blackgutter Plantation
OLD MARL PIT
OLD MARL PITS
Longlands Pool
Hobfield Lane
Rises
Oakley's Plantation
Mack's Plantation
Beacon Bank Farm
OLD MARL PIT
Woodhill Lane
Radmore Lane
RADNORE WOOD
Radmore House
Allotment Gardens
OLD MARL PIT
Schoolhouse Lane

CHAPTER TWO

The search

We were now set fair to choose a place to settle down. This need no longer be within easy reach of a large town for we preferred somewhere too isolated to attract competition from wealthy commuters. The fact that we might be snowed in for a week at a stretch would not matter to me because I can write as easily peering over a snowdrift as if the fields around are bathed in sunshine. Luckily for me, my wife is also fond of quiet places.

We didn't mind an old house nor were we wedded to all mod cons. Our previous experience had taught us that good septic tanks are no worse than sewage schemes designed for communities and that there are very few places out of reach of electricity.

Our last house had been on the edge of a village with a ring of public footpaths round the field and orchard. We had been greatly troubled there by village cats which hunted our ornamental waterfowl and pigeons and wild birds, so that I grew to regard cats as worse vermin than carrion crows or foxes. This time we would try to find somewhere less likely to be plagued by cats or trespassers. It might even come for a song since advantages in our eyes might seem disadvantages to others and put our competitors off.

We put our names on the books of every estate agent for miles around saying that we thought the ideal place might be a small run-down farm of marginal land.

I would have neither the time nor the experience to make a farm pay but I wanted as much land as I could get for my money, with the greatest possible variety of terrain. A derelict farm, on marginal land, seemed a far better bet than a potentially profitable place which would fetch a mint of money.

Our search soon rubbed in the fact that most farmers are too practical to worry about aesthetic values. Farm buildings were stark and their surroundings usually treeless. However beautiful the distant view, the house always seemed to overlook the muckyard and the only things in the garden were cabbages and sprouts.

When we did find a place we liked on the edge of Blithfield Reservoir, the South Staffordshire Waterworks, who were selling it, had reserved the shooting rights so that we could have done nothing to stop gangs of trigger-happy cowboys shooting everything which moved although we owned the land. There was also eighteen inches of water in the cellar, which didn't add to its charms.

We discovered delightful houses with main roads running right up to the door or with cottages near enough to dissect the seat of every family row. Some of the nicest places were in the centre of estates but were only to let and not for sale, and almost invariably their sporting rights had been retained by the owner or let to a syndicate, which would have been far worse.

Our inspections ranged from Worcestershire to Derbyshire and Shropshire to Leicester. They were all either too much money, or jigsawed by public footpaths or devoid of trees and cover, subject to flooding or otherwise beset with snags.

We searched particularly closely between Cannock Chase and Needwood Forest because the whole area has always been owned by a few families possessing great estates

The lands of the Earl of Lichfield and Sir Charles

Wolseley stretched to the Bagot Estate at Abbot's Bromley and the Earl of Shrewsbury at Ingestre. Between them, the Bagots and the Meynells and the Queen's Duchy of Lancaster estates at Marchington covered most of the ancient forest of Needwood. This whole stretch of unspoilt country is about as big and almost as well wooded as the Dukeries in Nottingham. A marvellous place to sink our roots.

The reason that it has not been developed is that the great families which owned it had taken care that it was unsullied by industry so that almost the only employment available was farm labouring or other work on the estates. Until cars replaced horses it was difficult to travel daily to towns for a job and even now a large part is outside comfortable commuting distance to any choice of jobs.

Although the area was ideal from our point of view, it proved very difficult to find what we wanted. Those who own large estates would be stupid to ruin them by selling off odd parcels of land in the middle.

We gradually narrowed our search to the area round Lord Bagot's estate at Abbot's Bromley. About six centuries ago the de Blithfields and the Bagots united when the Bagot of the day married 'the girl next door', as the present Lady Bagot puts it.

'Next door' is a relative term. The houses were in fact about a couple of miles apart, each on its own land but the two estates became one when their owners were wed. After that they lived at Blithfield, which was the better house, and for centuries were able to drive across their land, now covered by the top half of Blithfield Reservoir, up into Bagot's Park, more than three miles away.

There was about a thousand acres of parkland here and a thousand acres of Bagot's Wood without an important house because the owners had chosen to live on what used to be the adjoining estate of Blithfield. All that remains of the original Bagot home is a stone monument by an ancient moat at Bagot's Bromley.

The deer fence round Bagot's Park was maintained intact until the last war and it held a herd of fallow deer, a herd of red deer and the famous herd of Bagot goats. An old agent told me that, seventy years before, the Lord Bagot of the day had said, 'Neighbour, the park fence is beginning to creak. Put another one up.' 'He little knew what he asked,' said the agent. 'It took three men three years, for it was five miles long.' All the oak for it was felled and cloven on the estate and the magnitude of the task is some measure of the scale on which the great families lived and thought in those days.

The park was mainly rough, feggy grazing with sprawling patches of bracken and rushes and scattered groves of ancient oak trees, mostly past their prime and stag headed. During the war the War Agricultural Executive Committee insisted that the herd of goats be cut down in size and the park ploughed and seeded for grazing. This was impossible where there were too many roots so that the least productive parts were allocated for a practice bombing range.

The goats would have probably have been liquidated altogether if they had not been a unique herd whose ancestors had been presented to the Bagot family by King Richard II six hundred years before, and there was a legend that when the last goat went the Bagot family would die out.

Such continuity was one of the things that we were fighting to preserve and the goats had survived plenty of wars before, so a nucleus was reprieved and spent their war wandering in Bagot's Wood.

After the war Bagot's Wood was felled, except for about eighty acres, and replanted by the Forestry Commission, mainly with Corsican Pines and other softwoods. The estate had been gradually shrinking for more than a century, partly due to death duties and other taxation, and partly because the second Lord spent a fortune enlarging and altering his great house at Blithfield. He also built a stone cottage with oak plank facing at the entrance to Bagots Park which would cost a king's ransom in craftsmanship today and must have set his lordship back a pretty penny even in the good old days a century and a half ago.

It is called Goat Lodge and has a massive stone porch topped by seven goat's heads, carved in solid stone, and the stone crest and coat of arms of the Bagot family. The chimney is a massive stone structure with carved deer heads at the top and stone arrows pointing down each corner. There is a stone bow and two quivers of arrows over the main window and the carved oak barge boards are superb.

It was easy enough to explore the whole district around because the man who rented Bagots Park from the owners sublet the grazing on a seasonal basis. Farmers could send cattle and sheep to graze there for a few shillings a week and the whole mixed herd was supervised by a stockman who lived in Squitch house, the only cottage in the park.

Scores of people used to wander about and simply say they had come to see how their cattle were doing if they were challenged. Or that they had come to see a friend's cattle for him. As there were upwards of thirty genuine owners, it was impossible to check the truth of their stories so the whole place was crawling with trespassers.

Some even came to look at their cattle with guns under their arms—and went home with a pheasant or a hare in their pockets. Others arrived with spades to steal turf for their lawns or to dig up wild daffodils or primroses for their gardens.

The park dropped away to the north east to a small farm of about seventy acres in the valley beyond the Bagot

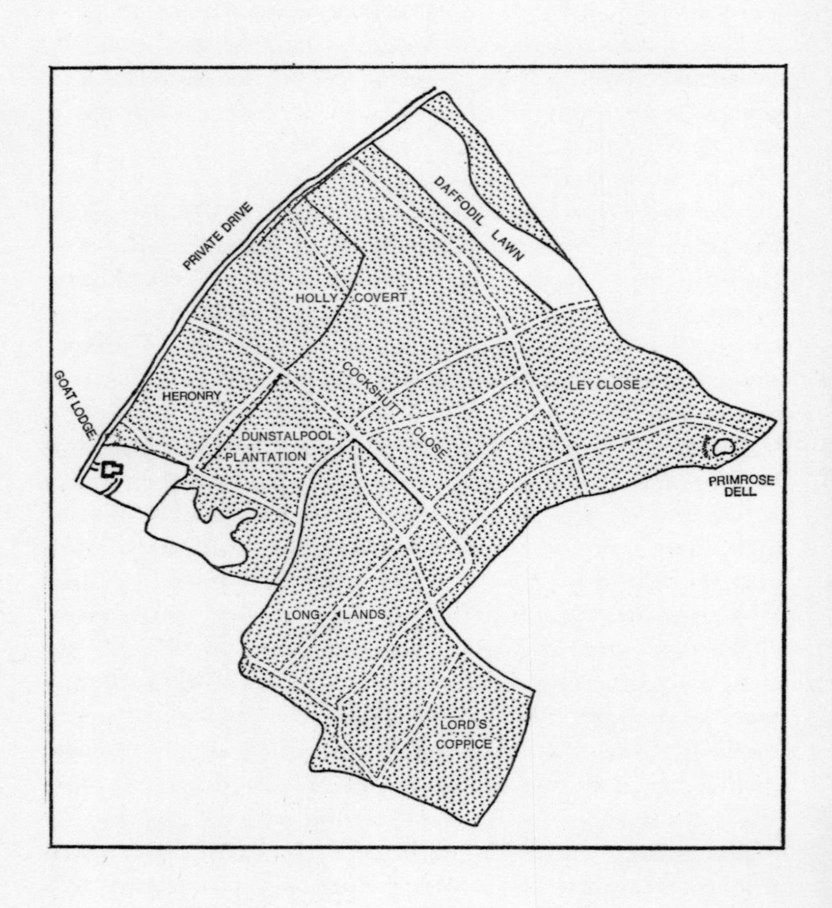
PRIVATE DRIVE
DAFFODIL LAWN
HOLLY COVERT
GOAT LODGE
HERONRY
COCKSHUTT CLOSE
LEY CLOSE
DUNSTALPOOL PLANTATION
PRIMROSE DELL
LONG LANDS
LORD'S COPPICE

boundary. The house was small and low and half timbered and full of character. A few yards of garden sloped down to a strong stream fed by springs a quarter of a mile away in the wood.

The cowsheds abutted the house and could easily have been incorporated in it to make a home of sensible size, while a few hours' work with a bulldozer would have dammed the stream to make a most beautiful pool in the valley bed below the house.

There were snags by urban standards. The farm was at the dead end of a lane and drive almost two miles from the village so that, in deep snow, escape would be impossible by car and difficult on foot. That was the least of the worries for there is nothing better than a snow drift to deter competitors and deflate the price.

Water was piped from a spring on someone else's land so that the purity and continuity of supply might have posed more serious problems. And the only sanitary arrangements consisted of an earth closet at the bottom of the garden. However picturesque its curtain of honeysuckle might be in summer, this promised cold comfort in winter slush and snow.

We worried about none of these things. There was electricity for light and cooking and if all the other modern conveniences had been installed, the price would doubtless have been beyond our pocket.

The greatest advantage was that the house was empty and the farm apparently pretty derelict. Whenever we had a spare half-day, my wife and I trespassed there and smoked pipe dreams about minor alterations which would transform it to Utopia.

One day we found a lad scything thistles there who told us that the owner farmed a dozen or so miles away on the edge of Cannock Chase. I dug him out and we nearly did a deal but it never quite came off.

A few months previously the Sixth Lord Bagot had died and most of the estate had been sold to an undisclosed buyer who was trying to resell it again by splitting it up. He was said to live in the Bahamas and had bought the whole 2,300 acres except for Blithfield Hall and its grounds, which Nancy Lady Bagot owned in her own right, and Goat Lodge, which had been withdrawn from the original sale.

I had had my eye on Goat Lodge for a long time, but my wife wouldn't hear of it. It had been empty for two years and the yard was head high in nettles, which almost obscured the outbuildings. There was a pig sty, coalshed, earth closet and wash house, with a pump outside to fill the copper and the sink with water from the well.

The fact that the pump didn't work was of no great importance because the house had lately been connected to piped water and boasted a stark cold tap in the scullery. This was over an earthenware sink which emptied through a pipe in the wall, spilling directly on to the garden because there was no drain to which it could be connected.

'Garden' flattered the patch outside the house. Miss Mary Jackson, the last tenant, had been born there but spent her middle years as lady's maid to the family at their London house and had come back to Goat Lodge in her declining years.

The Bagot Goats had been her love in life and this affinity had encouraged them to make the woods around her house their headquarters. Goats are browsing creatures and they don't graze off sweet pasture short, as sheep would do, but wander on taking a mouthful here and a mouthful of what they fancy there. They are fond of broad-leaved plants and shrubs and the bark of trees, so that they had eaten their way through Mary's holly hedge and then demolished the contents of her garden.

By the time we had got to know the district well, Mary had grown old and retired to an old people's home. The cottage windows had been boarded against vandals and the goats had left nothing in the garden but a jungle of thorny scrub.

This complete dereliction in the garden put my wife off most but the house was not encouraging. From the outside it was very imposing despite the wilderness of weeds and overgrown wood surrounding it, giving it such a dark and sinister air. I should never have been surprised to see a coven of misshapen naked witches dancing at dusk around the door.

The inhospitable dearth of conveniences within were mitigated by the wonderful stone carvings on the chimney and over the window and porch, and by the timeless craftsmanship of the dowelled oak cladding.

It had been roofed with shingles instead of tiles and thousands of flies crept into the crevices to hibernate. The woodpeckers had discovered this and drilled scores of small holes through the top layer of shingles to gorge on the fat feast below. It was typical of the quality of craftsmanship that had been lavished on the place that even this did not make the roof leak.

The house was really a folly which had been built to lend splendour to the woods at the entrance to Bagots Park. Even in its decay it was easy to see visions of splendid carriages and beautiful women, escorted by their men, riding over from Blithfield to picnic in summer or to shoot or hunt in winter.

Nobody would care, a century and a half ago, if the humble goatherd who opened the gate and lived in such a splendid house, was short of comforts when the front door clanged behind him.

Clang is an understatement for the thunderous thump of that great door because it was fashioned from two-inch oak with enough wrought iron studs to do credit to a medieval castle portcullis. The wrought iron handle was heavy enough to serve as a knocker to recall the dead and the great steel latch slammed down with the finality of doom.

However effective that door was for keeping intruders at bay, it was a dead loss as a draught excluder. This was important because it opened directly into the living-room which was heated only by a tiny range with two ovens.

There was nothing else but a kitchen and tiny scullery and larder with three little bedrooms above. The back door opened directly out of the kitchen and it was necessary to mount an expedition and to battle through the nettle bed to reach the earth closet twenty or thirty yards away across the yard.

The edge of Bagot's Wood had crept across what was once the orchard to merge with the cottage garden and there was a cattle pasture to the south bordered by such a high hedge that it was impossible to see whether cattle were grazing there or not. The quiet was so deep that you could hear their harsh tongues rasping at the grass although you only knew by guesswork where they were.

A rough drive to the cottage potholed on through the wood to the farm in Bagot's Park and there was so much scrub at the side of it that it was as shady as the banks along a Devon lane. The woods behind seemed to stretch to infinity. A large part of them, getting on for nine hundred acres, had been felled and replanted by the Forestry Commission, but eighty acres to the North East of the cottage still stood.

This was of no great economic value. It was mixed oak and sycamore and elder and birch and nut and ash which gave a wonderful variety of food and cover. It was a mixture which is growing rarer in England because such trees are too often replaced by the miserable sterility of get-rich-quick conifers.

It wasn't the beauty of the place which seduced me, for it is neither very beautiful nor pretty. Yet I knew in my bones that the more intimately I got to know it, the deeper I should fall in love.

The nearest roads were a mile to the south and two and a half miles to the north while the two local railway stations were six miles away, one at Rugeley and the other at Uttoxeter. There was solace and seclusion here from the score years when I had never been able to retreat from crowds, although I was quite aware that old acquaintances would shudder at the thought of being so buried alive.

The baker and butcher and milkman wouldn't call and it would be easy enough to be cut off from the world by either snow or fog, but we saw far more immediate snags than that. The cottage garden was only half an acre and the adjacent woodland was up for sale as standing timber. The terms of the felling licence stipulated that the Forestry Commission would take it over as tenants when it had been felled and replant it with softwoods.

If that happened the poor little cottage would be left alone standing stark but not proud on the edge of a desert. When the young pines did eventually throw a protective cover over the mutilated woodland bed, the density of their canopy would stifle every other living thing.

It was plain that if we wanted the cottage it was vital to buy the adjacent woodland, if only to stop it being felled. The snag was that the man who owned the wood did not own the cottage, which had been withdrawn from the sale, presumably because the new Lord Bagot, who lived in Australia, wanted to keep at least a toehold in this country when he had disposed of the rest of the estate.

The wood was worth even less to us without the house to live in than the cottage would have been without the wood, so we tried for the cottage first.

Lord Bagot's agents said that it was not for sale but that he might let it to us at a low rent if we agreed to pay for major improvements and repairs. We would have been prepared to do this provided that we could get a lease longer than our expectation of life. When our heads had ceased to ache, it would be no hardship to us if our home was returned to its previous owner. But the agents' idea of a long lease was twenty-one years and neither of us reckoned to tumble off our perch so soon.

We screwed them up to fifty years if we spent a couple of thousand pounds on improvements, so we asked them to hold the deal on ice while we approached the gentleman in the Bahamas about buying part of his wood. He too was dealing through agents so that every letter took weeks to percolate through to someone who could make a decision.

It developed into a nightmare game of snakes and ladders. One day we were convinced it was all over bar the final signature, the next throw of the dice slithered us down the ladder to the start again.

We had Goat Lodge all but sewn-up when Lord Bagot thought this brother in England might like it for a weekend cottage. When we thought arrangements for the wood were complete, the vendors stepped the price up again. By the time His Lordship's brother decided he didn't want it, a stranger who kept a pub had raced in from obscurity to lead the field.

This waste of time allowed half the standing timber to be felled so that the wood which started as eighty acres dwindled to forty with the rest let to the Forestry Commission, condemned to be replanted at a confiscatory rent of half a crown an acre.

Whoever has tried buying a house knows the complications which can arise before buyer and seller and their solicitors conducting mysterious 'searches' can agree.

When the principals are scattered round three sides of the globe, the odds against making the transactions coincide escalate to the astronomical. We got so fed-up with the whole thing that we often felt like putting a match to all the papers though our determination not to take 'No' for an answer eventually paid off.

My solicitor rang up one day to say that he had got all the right signatures on all the right documents and he was delighted to say that Paradise was ours.

CHAPTER THREE

Shadows

Our Paradise in prospect proved to be a wilderness. For the years while I had worked for other people I had day dreamed of being my own boss. I had lived in the cloud cuckoo land where it was safe to say what one thought to those in authority. I had imagined some ideal state where faceless check numbers are treated with dignity and clocks would be cut down to size.

I had burned my boats when I decided to earn my living with my pen instead of only writing for a hobby, but I avoided getting scorched by cutting my needs to fit my assets. A few good broadcasts or articles in a week sent us lashing out to paint the town. In the lean patches we convinced ourselves that life could be as pleasant on bread and cheese of one's own as on somebody else's velvet expense account.

While I had spent my days sitting on a plush seat on the Board it hadn't been difficult to accumulate a layer of financial fat. Now that I was committed to buy Goat Lodge and the land around it I had to face the fact that if the ink dried in my pen I should have no alternative but to dig into my reserves till I was squeezed through the doors of the labour exchange.

It was my first real taste of insecurity. I had always had a regular salary and, however common it is for ambitious men to climb to success over the bodies of their fellows, the sort of old fashioned firm I had worked for did not sack old employees except for dishonesty or chasing the typist round the desk.

As a self-employed writer there was no dole and if I didn't work I shouldn't eat, and few employers would be interested in fresh labour as long in the tooth as fifty.

I took a hard look at the assets I had contracted to buy, which I hoped would be the raw material for a great deal of writing. Daffodil Lawn was the narrow, rushy swampy field farthest from the house between the wood and the park. It was about seven acres and the Bagot goats seemed to like it for they spent much of their time there, though I couldn't see that the dry wiry grass could do them much good.

Next to the lawn there was about forty acres of mixed hardwood and another forty where the trees had been sold but not all felled. The pitiless yowl of chain saws shattered what should have been peaceful silence here and drove most of the wildlife out. Although the land belonged to us, the man who had bought the timber had twelve months to get it out.

At the house end of the wood there had once been an orchard opening from the cottage garden but that had degenerated into a jungle of self set apple and damson and crab, even wilder than the garden. This was exactly to the taste of the goats which had ring barked most of the trees, leaving their skeletons standing stark and rotten.

Our greatest disappointment was the pool. A neck of the wood jutted out about eighty yards from the cottage to end in a lovely pool of an acre and a half, with sphagnum moss and rushes and bog bean and swamp at the edge. This was Dunstal Pool and, since it was fenced from the field on the farm side and open to the wood, we assumed we had bought it with the wood.

We wandered round it, calculating how many ornamental duck it would harbour and what varieties of wild fowl they were likely to attract. The land below the Hall at Blithfield had been flooded to make the reservoir which is about nine miles round and it has made one of the best wintering grounds for wildfowl in England. Tens of thousands of duck congregate there, floating in rafts in the centre of the water, far out of gunshot range from the banks.

When dusk falls they fly out on to the stubbles and other feeding ground for miles around, exploring every tiny pithole in their search for a variety of food. The birds themselves make a reservoir as inexhaustible as the water in the great lake and it was obvious that, if I threw food into Dunstal Pool and didn't disturb it, there might soon be a lovely mixed flock within a stone's throw of the house.

When I mentioned it to the agent, he blandly informed me that the pool was not included in the eighty acres I had bought. It belonged to the farm down the lane and the farmer had fenced his side simply to prevent his cattle getting bogged and their udders plastered with mud.

This time we were in luck. The farmer was about to retire and sell his farm so he let me buy the pool and an acre of paddock before he put the rest on the market. This really did make all the difference because there was no longer a neck of the woods jutting out. The whole place was now nicely rounded off so that we could walk out of the cottage over our own land right round the pool and into the wood.

Goat Lodge is on the schedule of houses of historic or architectural interest and I knew that planning permission to alter it might not be easy. Anyone who has had experience with bureaucratic bumbledom will know it is rarely easy to get planning permission for anything at all. I was told that plans to alter houses of architectural interest are not controlled by local councils but have to be passed by planners in London who are even more remote and awkward.

Once more we were lucky. However pleasant it looked to outsiders, the comforts were spartan by any standard. The front door opening into the living-room and the back into the kitchen let through enough draught to sail a toy boat when everything was battened down against the storm.

There was no drainage, no electricity, no bath, tiny windows and the earth closet was too near the well for my peace of mind. Unless someone was prepared to spend money on the place, it would obviously fall down with neglect. Since historic houses in ruins reflect no credit even on bureaucracy, they were prepared to allow additions to make the place habitable.

Horace Deakin produced the first plans on the back of a cigarette packet. Horace was a builder I had known for some years and he specialised in repairing old buildings. He was too much of a craftsman to put up with lazy or slap-dash hired labour, so he only worked with his father.

He was such a rarity as to be an anachronism who put craftsmanship before all else. Although he wasn't fast, he worked long hours and had few overheads so that his prices were competitive. When his jobs were done, they would obviously stay done for a very long time.

We paid an architect to translate Horace's plan from its cigarette packet to the complicated blueprints required by officials before they will so much as take their hands out of their pockets.

Then we bid him adieu for I knew Horace didn't like 'theory men, the newspaper and bowler hat brigade' as he called them, and it was obvious they would never have worked in double harness. At the first difference of opinion Horace would have put his case in highly unprofessional language.

The first thing to come on the site was a bulldozer to level the foundations and while it was on the job, we got it to clear the scrub from the garden and the rushes from the near side of the pool. The spot where Jess aimed to put her cherished plants was a tangle of shattered roots sticking out of holes like bomb craters. It needed greater faith than mine to visualise order ever emerging from such chaos.

I decided that the best way to help her would be to employ a team of gardeners. It was obviously such a tough assignment that it would break the backs of elderly, conventional sons of the soil, so I decided to do the thing big. I decided that my gardeners would be young, strong and literally live on the job till it was done.

The first thing Horace did was to put up an agricultural shed about thirty feet long by eighteen deep. This was to be the store for his building materials, a place to keep the tractor and, when he had done, a garage for the cars. So I asked him to partition one section off, in the meantime as sleeping quarters for the gardeners.

Fifteen of them arrived, and I didn't hire them but bought them from a friend who bred pigs. They were pedigree Large Whites and they arrived as young gilts of twelve weeks old. We made a wire netting pig run, opening out from the tractor shed so that they had the freedom of the whole area my wife had earmarked for her garden and no gardeners ever worked such long hours or attacked their task with such loving zest.

First they ate everything green which dared to poke its nose above the soil and, since nothing grew there but weeds, this was precisely what we wanted. When they had filled their bellies with easy pickings, they set about the hard stuff. Their powerful snouts were more effective than little crowbars at levering out the saplings so that all that was left for them to do was to turn up all the roots the bulldozer had loosened. When that was done they turned the pure soil over and over in their search for the diminishing returns of their labour, and most of what they ate reappeared later as rich and fragrant pigmuck.

Those fifteen pigs had the freedom of our garden for about five months and, when they had done the soil was as weedfree and well manured as a prize allotment. All that was necessary when they had gone was to hire a rotavator to finish the job they had started so that my wife could pop in her treasured possessions from her last garden.

The labour cost of the whole project was less than nil. As each gilt grew old enough, I introduced her to a pedigree boar and sold her about four months later when she was heavy in-pig and close to profit. So our gardeners lived full and free lives, rooting in the open as pigs so love to do instead of cooped in sties or broiler houses. At night they croodled up together, warm and snug, in deep straw after their evening meal of pig nuts which Horace put down for them when he finished his day's work. They were the only gardeners I ever had which showed a profit when they left.

Meanwhile Horace and his father got on with the house. The idea was that they should add a bathroom and bedroom upstairs and sitting-room, study and kitchen downstairs. This entailed pulling the old kitchen and tiny bedroom above it down and the whole operation took about nine months to complete.

The creative excitement as the sketch on the cigarette packet blossomed into reality was almost unbearable, but it had its worries too. Nothing ever seems to turn out as cheap as one hopes and this was no exception. Unforeseen tasks kept cropping up so that it was easy in moods of pessimism to be convinced that the whole project was stupid speculation and that, when it was done, my overheads would be too top heavy to balance on my pen.

In such moods the embryo garden was dull as a newly ploughed field, the pool a muddy swamp, half the wood was a stricken wreck and the house a cold and characterless shell.

I had never seen mud like that clammy clay, churned into black blancmange by builders' lorries and even the trees in the half wood we had saved looked stag-headed when they took their leaves off. What fools to stake our future on this infertility, to swap security for this perilous pig-in-a-poke.

No psychologist could prescribe a cure for such moods of black despair as certain as a lonely walk in my wilderness. Within seconds it was easy to get far enough into the wood to be out of sight of the house and the hammering which nagged my ears because I knew that every noisy blow was a penny bouncing out of my pocket.

Once in the wood, things were as they were a generation ago and would be, I hoped, a generation hence. The wind whispered so gently that it made the sound of a grey squirrel's claws, scuffling for grip on a silver birch, seem a loud obtrusive noise.

The best way to see things of interest was not to walk about but to lean against the trunk of a tree, to camouflage my dreadful human silhouette, and to remain there perfectly still.

The first time I tried this, a long tailed woodmouse watched me for a few seconds from the shelter of a bramble clump but forgot I was not part of the scenery almost at once. Then he carried on the important work that I had interrupted.

He was collecting acorns and storing them under the trunk of a fallen oak. However simple this may sound, it was hard work to him. The acorns were buried under layers of fallen leaves and there were no easy ones left. Pigeons and pheasants had skimmed the cream off the crop, which had shrunk to the dimension where nothing good comes easy. So the woodmouse kept shooting off in short darting sallies, stopping to sniff in the leafmould every foot or so.

His trouble was that he couldn't really keep his mind on the job. His huge ears kept twitching, as sensitive as radar scanners, and his great bulbous black eyes seemed incapable of focusing on the acorns beneath his feet lest an enemy crept up while his attention wavered.

Half of his mind was constantly watching and sniffing and listening for enemies. A stoat might be behind every root or a hawk or owl on every branch, when it would be a question of which reflexes acted first, the hunter's or the hunted.

Within seconds he had written me off as safe as a dead log, and he was running over my feet as freely as if they were no more than a jagged bottle left by a vandal out for a picnic. If he thought at all, I suppose he realised that I was far too clumsy and slow to do him any mischief so that he was wiser to concentrate on his natural, more deadly foes. This gave me a wonderful chance to observe him. I was close enough to see him freeze in his tracks, with his nose testing the air for danger, before he started to dig.

Although the leafmould was so soft, it was obviously quite hard work by a mouse's standards. The skin over his shoulders rippled as gracefully as the knotted muscles of a weightlifter and every time he unearthed his treasure trove he staggered with it to the fallen trunk and disappeared from view to put it into storage.

The whole episode took, perhaps, ten minutes though I hung about watching for a sequel and thinking about it for far longer than that. It was nothing rare and would not have excited professional biologists, nothing dramatic or spectacular, but that few minutes, watching a humble woodmouse stocking his larder for the winter restored my confidence. Penny hammer blows, mounting into pounds shrunk to their perspective. I knew no more what the future held than that mouse did. And suddenly I didn't care.

Having time to waste, my friends might think, in watching domestic chores of such a common creature suddenly mattered more to me than calculating economies in a factory production line to swell faceless profits by thousands of pounds. It was at last possible to shuffle priorities into the right order to put my theories into practice and it tasted very sweet.

The next things which fascinated me about my new found wilderness were not living creatures but inanimate words. The large-scale ordnance map, with twenty-five inches to the mile, showed every ride and clearing, every rise and hollow and patch of water on the surface of the wood and some of the drains under it.

Not only did it show the physical features but the names by which they were known as well. The house is labelled Woodman's Cottage—even humbler than Goat Lodge—and the stand of woodland next to it is Dunstal Pool Plantation, with Dunstal Pool where the wood ends. Dunstal Pool Plantation runs on into Holly Covert which joins up with Daffodil Lawn on the opposite side to the park.

That was the extent of the standing timber for the rest of the wood had either been felled or was still writhing under the axes of the timber fellers.

The map didn't recognise this, for maps are only wise after the event. This was but a transitory malady, for the Forestry Commission, who had taken a lease, would soon reclothe it, if only with miserable foreign pines, far inferior to the English oak and beech which grew there before.

The area which had been felled started at Ley Close,

ran through Cockshutt Close, Longlands and finished in Lord's Coppice, behind Dunstal Pool from the house.

It was a tremendous thrill to own a bit of England, important enough to have earned a permanent place on the map, with the house and each compartment of woodland recorded for posterity. Men had planted and named these woods long before we were born and, when we are long forgotten, the house and woods and pool will still be clearly marked for all to see.

It was not as some hollow status symbol that I valued it, but for completely different reasons. The pleasure it gave me, and the excitement, was because it was symptomatic, not of success or security since it could easily mean the reverse, but of continuity. I had suddenly acquired a place which I might leave better than I found it. I could play an active part in moulding the character of the countryside I loved so much.

The first nine months, while Horace and his father were building the extension, was a wonderful time of exploration. We were living ten miles away but I came over most days, ostensibly to settle snags that arose in the alterations. The experience I had had in charge of the production of a large factory had taught me to improvise and not easily to take No for an answer, but it had been experience of bigger gangs of men led, and often misled, by shop stewards bent on mayhem. I had never worked so closely with a craftsman before, who valued the quality of his work higher than the price he was paid for it.

I saw part of almost every course of bricks laid down and watched a roof put on which was as strong as the ribs of a sailing ship. There wasn't an electric junction box nor a central heating pipe joint which didn't have a loose board above it which could be opened as easily as a trap door in time of trouble.

Horace said that, as he knew who would be the mug

who would have to do any subsequent repairs, he was only making life easy for himself. I knew that the real reason was that he had always dreamed of building a house which would stand as a memorial when he was gone and that he would have nothing to do with work that was 'codged'.

He fitted the water tanks in the roof with control valves so that, when they eventually did canker through, they could be isolated and replaced without spilling a drop. We had lots of fun in the kitchen because one of the few things I enjoyed about Industry was applying the principals of Work Study. So we put in a central table with boarded sides to make a cupboard for ironing kit and bolted the whole contraption to the floor. Its size and position were arranged according to the relatively new fangled science of ergonomics, which is a fancy name for the common sense that has always tried to take the irk out of work.

We mounted this table the right distance from the stove and sink for food and pans to be transferred simply by pirouetting the body instead of jazzing about all over the room. And we put the store cupboards at the same distance on the other side of the table to assemble the ingredients of a meal precisely where they were needed with the minimum of effort.

The table being bolted to the floor meant that it was possible to bring an electric lead through the floor under the table and to mount a power point under the table top. A mixer or iron could then be plugged into this with no risk from loose cables trailing all over the floor.

It was not only to burnish the rust off my old industrial skills that I visited Horace so often. As it usually only took a few minutes to settle the latest batch of queries, as soon as I could I sneaked out into the wood to take the dogs for a walk and to surprise whatever, or whoever, I found there.

We had five dogs when we came. Jade and Mandy were two lurchers, bred for generations for gypsies who valued their brains as much as their skill at catching rabbits and hares for the pot. I also had Gypsy, who was an older lurcher, but faster and tougher and cleverer than any lurcher I ever owned. She was slightly smaller than the greyhounds who had contributed three quarters of her blood, with a harsh and wiry yellow coat, inherited from old fashioned deerhound blood somewhere deep in her ancestry.

Dinah was a whippet-lurcher who had really been pensioned off. Her sire was a successful racing whippet and her mother a cross between a whippet and a terrier, so she had three quarters of whippet blood in her veins. She was small and gentle though the years had skimmed the cream off her speed. So she let the faster dogs do the work but it was astonishing how often she managed to intercept their quarry by cunning anticipation. In the house she was affectionate and she always lay on the softest cushion in the room with such luxurious abandon that she had a flair for making the whole house seem comfortable and lived-in. Every dog we have becomes my favourite when his predecessors die, but Gypsy and Dinah stand out above most.

Our fifth dog was Tough, an alsatian I had bought as a pup from the County Police kennels when I did a television feature on police dog training there. Gypsies do not count taking a lurcher as stealing and, as lurchers tend to regard all the world as friends, it is a wise precaution to run a hard mouthed alsatian with them as an animated burglar alarm.

There is less danger of having one's wife stolen, but Goat Lodge is so isolated that a sharp dog, whose mother had caught and held a gamebagful of crooks, seemed likely to be as useful as ornamental. Taking all these dogs in the wood for a walk not only fizzed off some of their surplus energy but showed me all sorts of things I might not otherwise have seen. All the lurchers were working dogs and they caught a few rabbits in the parts of the wood where the timber fellers had cleared enough open space to get a fair run. It was hazardous work, though, because of the risk of hitting hidden tree stumps or branches grown over with bracken.

I have always enjoyed training dogs and take great pride in having a dog with me which is well behaved. So I found it a challenge to teach such old dogs new tricks by persuading them that they were not even allowed to chase rabbits until I gave the word.

Each time I went out, I chose a different route. By this means I gradually learned which clumps always had a pheasant hiding under them, which trees held squirrel dreys and where the rabbits bolted to. Several times I saw a fox, which was such a temptation to the dogs that nothing would prevent them giving chase unless I had seen it in time to make them lie down before it came into their sight. Their natural antipathy was so strong that it was almost beyond them to resist such temptation and if once they started no power on earth would halt them. It was no good getting cross about this because I had always been so proud of Gypsy, who had often caught and killed one single handed.

But so long as I was alert enough to see their quarry before they did, they would drop at a flick of my finger and the cover was often so high that they never got a view and so were not tempted. This once gave me the chance to study the hunting techniques of a vixen catching field voles on Daffodil Lawn. She was mincing along, back slightly arched, with ears alert for the slightest rustle in the grass. From time to time she would stop and crouch in a catlike pose so still that she almost seemed to stop breathing.

Then she leaped quite high in the air so that she descended vertically on to the target she had located more by ear than by sight. Her judgement seemed infallible, though she sometimes had to scratch below the surface when her quarry was lying up in the illusory safety of its nest.

The wind was right, from her to us, but it amused me to see her concentration, which blinded her to the fact that she had a human enemy and five fast dogs within eighty yards or so.

We saw badgers on evening walks, when we came over after supper without the dogs, and hares and fallow deer and hedgehogs and stoats, but one of my keenest delights was the song of the grasshopper warblers which lived in the short stuff the timber fellers had left on Ley Close and Cockshutt Close.

The time to enjoy them best was just around dusk. Tree pipits sing there all day, flying high into the air and trilling as they descend as steep as parachutes. But when evening comes, the tree pipits quieten and lazy wood pigeons doze into silence, leaving the grasshopper warblers to hold the field.

They have been singing their continuous buzzing melody all day, but it is only at the stillness of dimmity that the tiny birds can really make themselves heard.

Time was when I would cheerfully have chosen a holiday hotel simply on the chance of the pleasure of seeing and hearing them. Now I could hear them on my own doorstep and, when the extension to the house was complete, I should have the privilege of hearing them any time I took an after supper stroll!

In many ways the herons have given me more pleasure

than any birds in the wood. There had been a heronry in Bagots Wood, across the drive from us, for more generations than anyone could count.

They build huge nests in colonies, like rooks, and often add year by year to these old nests until the ungainly bundles could be cart loads of twigs cascaded from the sky into the treetops. The Bagots Wood heronry had contained about forty-four nests in its heyday, and they could be seen from the main Uttoxeter–Abbots Bromley road.

The trees of Bagots Wood were sold in lots and felled between 1950 and 1958. By bad luck or bad management the woodmen came to fell the actual trees where the birds were nesting three times in seven years.

Herons are particularly shy birds. They have to be or they would long have been extinct because many fishermen and gamekeepers, who believe they have the right to kill everything which harms or even competes with their quarry, have no compunction about shooting rare birds.

The breeding results of the Bagots Wood herons slumped catastrophically for five or six seasons, because the disturbance at their nests was added to all the other hazards. The hard winter of 1962/63 was almost the last straw, but the instinct to preserve the species is indomitable and the survivors came over to our wood the year we bought it.

I found fourteen demoralised pairs which built their nests, scattered and haphazard, not in a colony but in odd ones and twos in Holly Covert and Dunstal Pool Plantation, which were now the only standing trees remaining from what had recently been a thousand proud acres.

This uncharacteristic dispersal of nests almost implied a conscious decision to spread the risk of having the trees cut down again while there were eggs or young in the nests. The lack of unity in repelling crows and other predators seemed the lesser of the evils.

There are only five heronries in the whole county of

Staffordshire, so I was delighted to welcome them and utterly determined that they should not be disturbed again if I could help it.

Whatever gift ungenerous Fate denied me, at least she endowed me with a pachydermous hide. My skin is so thick that I don't give a damn what anyone thinks. This proved a great asset because the wood was not only full of foxes and herons and woodland birds. At weekends it was often infested with trespassers who threatened to rid it of everything else by sheer pressure of humanity.

Mary Jackson, who had tended the goats and lived at Goat Lodge before us, had died two years before we came. Her father had lived here before her and I believe was Lord Bagot's last keeper and his brother was woodman.

At that time the gate across the drive had been kept locked and nobody got through without a key or written permit from Lord Bagot. The estate gradually fell into disrepair and the woodland fences decayed so that intruders could infiltrate from the rear.

Mary Jackson did her best long before her father died. She guarded the key to the gate jealously and one man told me that she chased him off with a garden rake because he wouldn't take her No for his answer.

Things became more and more impossible because it was difficult to prove that people who said they had come to look at their cattle were not really grazing tenants with permission to be there.

They didn't all come for the innocent pleasures of making love in the bracken or delighting their ears with birdsong. I caught one man digging turf for his lawn and plenty digging up primroses and daffodils by the roots. Some came with guns and rifles with which they shot at anything from wild pheasants and deer to the goat heads carved in stone above the porch. They came with dogs to hunt the hares and put bags of lime down the shaft of the

Author and Tick in ride opposite the house

Author, Tick and Spider at sitting-room window overlooking Dunstal Pool

Roe buck and doe feeding in front of sitting-room and study

The drive potholes on up into the Park. Author, Spider, Mandy, Tough, and Fly

The duck keep a patch of water free from ice on Dunstal Pool

Mandy, Fly and Spider, the lurchers, by the fire in the sitting-room we added

Roe buck at bird table by sitting-room window

Stone goats heads over the porch of Goat Lodge. 'Our Board of Directors' who never make a wrong decision.

Hall window which projects into bedroom above and has panes in cast iron frame instead of leaded lights

Lois Millar and Liz Moonie at Primrose Dell where they are doing work on conservation

Daffodil Lawn in Spring

Author and wife in garden, showing piece added on to house

Roe buck and doe come to bird table by window

Dunstal Pool and Countryside 1970 Award, presented by Prince Philip

pump in the yard, tipped rubbish and broken bottles in the wood and climbed the trees for herons' eggs or threw brick ends into their nests in bloody-minded vandalism.

Even the innocent ones did damage. Simply by walking in the wood while the herons were sitting, they scared the shy birds off their nests so that their eggs were eaten by crows before they plucked up courage to return.

No newcomer to a village is popular. Such strangers are natural objects of suspicion and the angel Gabriel wouldn't be accepted in our village for twenty years—and even then he wouldn't be 'one of us'.

So I reckoned I'd go the whole hog. It seemed more sensible to be written off as a brute, with some chance that people would relent when they discovered the reasons, than to start off friends with all the world but have to tighten up subsequently.

The whole thing was rather taken out of my hands when I received an invitation from the Head Mistress of the School of St Mary and St Anne to take supper with the staff and then to tell the girls what I intended to do.

I thought this might be a loaded question. The School of St Mary and St Anne is one of the largest girls' boarding schools in the country and Nancy Lady Bagot is on the Council. Not unnaturally, she had given the girls the virtual freedom of the estate. They could go almost wherever they liked.

Spread over a couple of thousand acres, this might scarcely be noticed. Certainly not at the Hall, which is three miles away on the other side of Blithfield Reservoir. But the possibility of a gaggle of five or six hundred schoolgirls in our wood terrified me. A swarm of locusts singing in concert with a murmuration of starlings would be sepulchurial silence by comparison.

I didn't disguise the fact that I intended to make the

woods into a sanctuary for birds rather than bird watchers and that I should try to keep the whole area as quiet as I could.

I had already explained politely to people I had found wandering about that I would rather they went somewhere else and most of them had been perfectly reasonable and understanding so that we had parted on amicable terms.

Others had exhibited varying degrees of resentment at not being allowed to wander where they considered they were doing no damage, whatever I might think. I explained to these, in words of whatever clarity it took to make my meaning plain, that I had worked hard to save the money to buy the place and sacrificed my security to live here. The reward I sought in exchange was to live among undisturbed wildlife with people of my own choice for company.

News of this forthright approach had apparently preceded me to the School of St Mary and St Anne. A dignified old lady stood up in the balcony and asked directly if my policy of seclusion for the birds meant exclusion for the girls.

I replied that, in general, it did but that I should be only too delighted to give any help I could to senior girls who were actively interested in natural history, but nobody accepted the invitation for several years.

Tough the alsatian virtually cleared the wood of less attractive visitors. It was not that she was savage because she never bit anyone, but she would bark on command and looked pretty formidable. I reinforced the effect of this by painting a highly coloured, if fictitious, picture of her exploits in the bar of the Goats Head Inn. She acquired such a reputation there that locals seemed to think she was more dangerous than a pride of lions loose in the wood.

CHAPTER FOUR

Substance

The move was both hectic and exciting. We had sold our last house with planning permission to build a number of new houses on the field between the house and the village and the new owner wasn't interested in the garden. He said my wife could take what plants and shrubs she liked with her.

Our pigs had put the ground in fine fettle. It was virtually weed-free and so fertile with pigmuck that all we had to do was to hire a rotovator and churn it up. A landscape gardener brought four lorry loads of shrubs from the last place and planted them in a couple of days with his gang of young labourers.

By the time we arrived she had created an instant garden. A yew hedge sloped down from the house to join a rhododendron hedge along the drive side and there was a short holly hedge to hide the greenhouse. She brought bamboos and azaleas, favourite shrubs with tongue-twisting names and a variety of crabs and cherries and ornamental trees. The job was finished off by sowing grass seed for the lawn.

Jess is so keen on her garden that the one thing which had clouded her joy at swapping our last place on the edge of a village for more land in deep country was the wrench of leaving her beloved plants.

When they were reprieved she grew visibly taller for it was the one thing necessary to make her as keen as I to come. She has devoted countless hours since to charming her garden out of the jungle she started with.

I on the other hand, am no gardener and I had no intention of getting involved in physical work which produces such slow results. My creed is that snow comes on its own in winter, and falling leaves in autumn but, if we have patience, the sun melts the snow and the rain rots the leaves to rich compost, all in good time. I would sooner see the yard ankle deep in golden leaves than try to out-Canute Canute with a broom.

It seemed sensible to make the kitchen garden the minimum size that would be functional. Vermin would scoff the lot from a big but unprotected cabbage patch before we were astir in the morning. My idea was to make what amounted to a fruit cage because I reckoned we should get a bigger crop that way from a smaller area.

We put up a framework about ten yards long and five wide, covered it with small mesh wire netting and we grow nothing there but strawberries, raspberries and the odd row of peas and beans.

Cohorts of wood pigeons and squirrels and blackbirds sit drooling with envy outside this cage and I take selfish delight in seeing they do not get a single berry. That kitchen garden is the best investment I ever made except, perhaps for the automatic dish-washing machine.

So, on the first night we moved in we could look out to the south and west on quite a respectable garden. Not then mature, of course, but the hedges and shrubs have grown in the meantime to a size which provides privacy from the prying eyes of strangers and nesting cover for a wide variety of birds. Which is all I ask of a garden.

I fell asleep to the background music of herons quarrelling in the wood. The early young, which were more than half fledged and insatiably hungry, kept up a clatter with their beaks as continuous as the hub-bub of a gaggle of typists trying to get home early.

This background noise was occasionally punctuated by eerie screams as if murder was being committed.

The explanation was less dramatic. Old herons were returning by the light of a full moon, weighed down by fish and frogs and water voles. They found it almost impossible to keep pace with the voracious appetites of their young, who shrieked with anticipation the moment they were silhouetted over the tree tops. The gurgling which followed when the old birds alighted would make the choking death rattles of strangulation sound tame by comparison.

The old birds thrust their dagger-like bills deep down their offsprings' throats and regurgitated their half digested fishy catch, provoking moans of masochistic satisfaction.

Sleep was impossible beneath such strange orchestration, but being kept awake proved to be delightful. 'Our' herons, in our wood, were going about their business as if we were not there. Till then, I had been happy to go miles to see a heronry and had often stood transfixed, marvelling at the skill of such dedicated fishermen.

The snag about going on expeditions to watch wildlife is that it is impossible to know if what one sees is just some lucky rarity or commonplace. And seeing nothing seems such a waste of time.

Now, for the first time, I was living amongst the things which fascinated me instead of simply visiting them. As I lay in bed, listening to those herons, I knew that I could watch their dark forms float across the window at first light, and possibly see them fishing in the pool. For the first time in my life, I could hear the dawn chorus of woodland birds from the comfort of my bed and, as the dawn broke, it would show me what came first into the woodland ride across the paddock.

'Ride' at the time, flattered it. The timber fellers had not yet finished in Lords Coppice and, when they had trimmed a trunk of branches, they hitched it behind a crawler tractor and 'snigged' it, or towed it, near to the timber drug for loading.

The drug they were using was not the old fashioned wooden chassis, with wheels located by a central pole, but a steel affair, designed to be dragged across rough country by a caterpillar tractor. Snigging large tree trunks, one after the other, cut great channels down the centre of the rides and the constant traffic carved deep ruts along the edges. So each ride was reduced to three parallel pools of mud with narrow lines of feggy grass between them.

Our soil is heavy, glutinous clay, which holds the water like a plastic sheet. 'Daggly' soil the woodmen called it, for drizzly days, in these parts, are daggly days. So going for a walk along the rides, when we first came, entailed picking our way across the daggly rits, or ruts, left where the woodmen had snigged their logs.

Not that this worried me. My standard footwear, since we came here, is rubber boots, and it would have been a pleasure to have ploughed through rits waist deep for the satisfaction of wandering through my own bit of England which is stuffed with such treasures.

Persuading myself that it was only until the novelty wore off, I wandered round the wood at least three times a day, whatever the weather.

After breakfast, or often before it, I went to feed the pigs in the run on the far side of the pool, where we had moved them when they were redundant as gardeners. Their numbers had dwindled, because I sold them about a fortnight before they were due to farrow, but the last two or three had proved difficult to get in-pig.

I have always liked pigs. I like the smell of them when they are healthy outside, though the stench of intensive pig units can be revolting. Despite their little eyes, they are extremely intelligent and affectionate so that I was always sorry to see them go because I wished them a good home as fervently as I would wish luck to a dog or horse.

They provided us with a lot of amusement too because one of them could escape from the safest enclosure as easily as Houdini and then her sisters followed. Dusk was just falling one day when Horace Deakin's father called down from the roof, where he was working, that he had just seen a strange woman in the wood. Then another and another, all with light coloured dresses on, he said. It turned out to be the pigs escaping once more and setting off, ghostlike across the ride, to root for acorns under the oak trees.

It would have been unthinkable, having fed them, not to have carried on round the wood 'on my way home'. Although there were only fourteen herons nests, that year, spread out down the length of the wood, the young birds were so voracious that the old birds seemed to commute unceasingly, laden with fish to feed them. But I think the most pleasant surprise in those first weeks, was the number of fallow deer in the wood.

I had often got up at dawn or stayed out till darkness fell, just on the offchance of seeing a wild deer on Cannock Chase. The idea of deer feeding freely, right up to the house, however commonplace it may be in good deer country, had never crossed my mind.

Although I did see plenty of deer, it was only fleeting views, because they were very wild indeed. They had to be because some of the local farmers had no compunction whatever in letting fly with a shotgun whenever they got within sight.

I soon discovered that a few handfuls of maize, scattered on the ride by the house lured them down at dawn and dusk. I could sit quietly on the terrace after supper or lie awake at first light and watch eight or ten fallow deer feeding on the corn I had offered them.

I was anxious to see what their reaction would be to deer of different species which they couldn't have seen before when they first saw Miss Roedoe, our hand-reared roe deer. She had arrived two years before as a kid and had been a real joy to rear on the bottle.

There is no way of getting to know a young animal more intimately or of establishing more mutual confidence than by rearing it so, and this young deer had grown into the most graceful sprite imaginable. Not wanting to risk her being shot or worried by farm dogs or foxhounds, I had fenced in a little over six acres, including the pool and the house, with six foot netting buried at the base. This was not only intended to prevent the dogs straying on to farmland or disturbing the wood, but to keep the roe deer in and to make a fox-proof haven where the wild ducks and pheasants could breed in peace.

It had been quite a problem to decide how to bring the deer over from her paddock, where she had been reared and had security. She was quite fearless with the dogs and us and she tolerated strangers very well up to the point when she feared they might surround her.

The instant the possibility of capture crossed her mind, she changed from an affectionate, tame inoffensive creature to a panicky wild animal.

I knew perfectly well that, if I picked her up, and stuffed her unceremoniously into a travelling crate, I might well lose her confidence for ever. Even worse she might fly into paroxysms of fear and injure herself in her struggles.

Her Achilles heel was greed. She simply could not resist chocolate digestive biscuit or flaked maize sprinkled with a little sugar.

Six weeks before we moved, I made a box, open at both ends, large enough for her to walk through like a tunnel.

I padded the inside very thickly with sacking stuffed like an eiderdown quilt with soft straw. I fed her each day nearer to this box until the food was placed inside. When she would feed freely from either end, I closed one end and started again. She objected to this at first because it was too great a threat to her security to risk going into a 'blind' passage. It seemed almost as bad as being surrounded by a circle of strange people, but there was one important difference. People could not keep as still as this box could.

It was the most patient Lady Bountiful of all time because any food I put inside it remained motionless there, tempting but harmless, till she plucked up the courage to tuck-in.

Long before we were ready to move here, I could bait the box at the blind end, farthest from the opening, and she would walk right inside to feed before I was out of sight. She did this once too often the morning the removal van arrived. In a couple of strides I had closed the door behind her and shut her in the box. Having been inside so often before, she took no apparent notice and we had put her on the van and set off for Goat Lodge before she realised anything was amiss.

The real test came when we arrived. I feared she would dash off madly the moment we let her out and that she would bang, full tilt, into the wire netting fence which was painted black to make it inconspicuous.

The danger when deer run headlong into wire netting is not so much that they will break their necks or legs but that they will hit the wire with their teeth hard enough to wrench them out.

We unloaded the crate as soon as the van arrived and set it down facing the pool. If she did stampede, it would do her less harm to get a ducking than to pile flat out into the netting.

I need not have worried. She looked around for a moment and then started to graze as if nothing unusual had happened. The journey didn't seem to have troubled her in the slightest, perhaps because six previous weeks feeding in her travelling case had endowed it with the look and scent of home. But I was lost in admiration for the way she stepped out, with all the aplomb of a prima donna receiving homage from her audience. We have much to learn from animals about accepting the inevitable with dignity.

After grazing for a few moments her curiosity overtook her greed. There was a good sweet clover in the paddock sward but this was the first time she had ever seen woodland—and roe deer instinctively seek thick cover and adore the broad leaves of honeysuckle and bramble and wild rose and hazel and the saplings of hardwood trees. They are not by nature grazing animals, like sheep, which will crop the turf short as a bowling green. Deer prefer to browse and to move quite quickly on, taking a mouthful of the best here and a few luscious leaves there but leaving the rest for lesser fry.

So my doe wandered casually off towards the wood, not hurrying but at a well mannered gait which allowed her to pick and choose the sweetest foliage as she passed. It was an object lesson in etiquette. Without ever seeming the least greedy, she managed to feast on the tit-bits until I thought she'd burst, but she did it so smoothly that, if my manners had been as good as hers, I should never have noticed. Cultured folk, well skilled at keeping the flow of good conversation going throughout the most appetising meal, would have turned green with envy.

However much she enjoyed her food, she never allowed it to interfere for a moment with what was really her top priority. She was in a strange place and, being a species which depends for its safety on flight, it was vital to know where escape was easiest and in which directions it might be impossible.

So she wandered on until she came to the wire netting fence and walked along its boundaries, abstractedly munching as she learned by heart the limitations of her territory.

When she knew the perimeter beyond which escape was impossible, she turned her attention inwards. She wandered round the pool, testing boggy patches for soundness and tasting yellow iris leaves as if by accident. She came up to the house and was obviously annoyed that some inconsiderate dolt had erected a fence between her and the garden. Then she criss-crossed the paddock until she had branded its exact topography on her mind and lay down to chew her meditative cud.

When we had finished supper, that first evening, we sat wearily by the window, mentally pinching ourselves to prove it wasn't some delightful dream. The surface of the pool was a kaleidoscope of continually changing patterns as the wild duck flew off to feed, or returned with bow waves larger, for their size, than a flotilla of seaplanes would make. Somewhere in the wood a tawny owl was hooting threats to mice and voles and we noticed for the first time what a large sky we had bought with our wilderness.

We are fairly high up, as Midland heights go, somewhere about five hundred feet above sea level, so there aren't any hills to block the view. Yet the only buildings we can see are the cow sheds of Dunstal Farm, a quarter of a mile down the drive, for the roofs of Abbots Bromley village are sunk in the valley out of sight. The hills of Cannock Chase are seven or eight miles to the south, with the Trent valley mercifully swallowing Rugeley. When we cleared the scrub we managed to leave a gnarled old hawthorn tree to obliterate the great cooling towers and chimney of the power station there so that our view over ten or twenty miles to the south and east manages to convey the illusion that time has stood still for a century or more. On the horizon Cannock Chase is just as it has always been, the evening sky arches to the same spot in infinity and the same silence is broken by the same sweet bird song which lilted here when our venerable old oaks were in their prime.

This impression of timelessness was suddenly crystallised when four fallow deer came out of the wood to feed in the ride. One second it was devoid of all life and the next their silent silhouettes had slid into the open.

We see them at all times of the day now that we have convinced them that we mean them no harm, but they were so persecuted before we came that those which didn't skulk in daylight hours were soon hanging up as venison.

These four does had come out to feed within fifty yards of where our roe doe was chewing her cud. They were the first other deer she had ever seen, though of a different species, and we were anxious to note her reaction. I had noticed that her ears had been flickering in the direction that interested her for some time and it was obvious that she knew something was stirring in the wood, though she showed no ill mannered curiosity. This directional listening is one of her most useful traits for us, because we are often forewarned of strangers' approach by watching the deer long before the dogs sense anything amiss.

She watched these four strange fallow does for a while without any apparent interest, rose to her feet for a leisurely stretch and ambled towards them. They glanced up for no more than a second and continued to feed as if nothing had happened.

When she got close to them it became obvious that they were not the centre of attraction. She was simply making certain that they had not found tasty food that she had not yet discovered. Otherwise they were mutually disdainful.

I have watched them together many a time since, often no more than a yard or so apart, with only the wire netting fence between them, but they cut each other dead with no sign of recognition.

Having stuffed the discovery in a pigeonhole of my mind, I turned to watch them feeding for the simple joy of seeing lovely things rather than in any spirit of scientific thirst for knowledge.

One of my luxuries is the best pair of German binoculars that I could buy for rather more money than I could afford. They are an extravagance which causes me no twinge of conscience. Not only do they magnify in size, giving the illusion that the object is ten times nearer than it is, they were fashioned with such artistry that they are capable of peering into fading light deeper than the human eye can see.

They brought these fallow deer from the shadows of the dusk a hundred yards away to within ten yards of the sitting room window, as if they were on a magic carpet. When they seemed almost within arm's reach, their dowdy camouflage shelled off to leave their subtle duns and fawns and greys so glossy and bright that their rippling muscles showed beneath. Their ears and tails flicked off most of the flies, but from time to time they stopped grazing to turn their heads and ease an itch with a delicately probing hoof.

I have got to know them since so well that I can tell a stranger as a shepherd sorts his sheep, because we are on such terms of mutual trust that they often allow me to approach close enough to enjoy them in the same detail with my naked eye.

Nothing will surpass the thrill of that night when I first saw 'our' deer on our land for long enough to watch the shadows stretch and engulf them despite the power of my binoculars, and it was only when I actually lived here that I realised how imperfectly I knew the land and what shared it with me.

While Horace and his father had been working here for the last nine months, I had taken every opportunity to walk round and to see what was there to be seen. But it is impossible to see a tithe of the potential by walking round.

When we settled here, I was often in the wood before breakfast and after supper, usually after lunch and at all sorts of hours besides. Perhaps the most important lesson was that animals and birds are even keener clock-watchers than we are. They may use the sun or dusk or hunger or thirst instead of chains of cogwheels in a clock, to pace them through their day, but they are slaves of habit as surely as commuters in a rural dormitory.

I soon discovered that the same group of pheasants emerged on to the ride to feed at the same place, at the same time, each morning, and that a dark, melanistic cock performed his toilet in a dustbath at the roots of the same hawthorn each day.

It was important not to walk near one boundary at noon, for fear of driving the pheasants over the boundary on to a neighbour's, but they soon sized me up too. They learned that I left a train of grain behind me so that clearings that were empty when I came, miraculously filled with feeding birds soon after I had passed.

The mallard were sitting when we moved in and one old duck had her nest under a holly in the drive. She flew over the house, feathers hunched and quacking irritably just as we were finishing breakfast. When she had eaten, she flew down to the pool, drank water as deep as a drunk-ard supping beer and splashed and bathed noisily. She obviously derived great satisfaction from giving irritable insect pests such a dowsing while working her stiffness off so pleasantly. Then she came out on to the bank and preened and groomed herself as meticulously as a debutante going to a ball.

The whole of this feeding and grooming routine took almost exactly three quarters of an hour, so that it was possible to predict her return to her nest as accurately as the time she would leave it. I found the knowledge invaluable in discovering the nests of all sorts of other birds which would have been impossible to find except by pure luck on a haphazard search.

As a boy I had systematically pried into hedges and thickets and the holes in trees or crevices behind loose bark. Practice had made me more perfect only to the extent that experience made me more observant and prompted me where I was most likely to be successful. But success or failure was still largely a matter of luck.

Now that I could wander over the same place so constantly, I noticed the same animals and birds regularly about the same areas. I often paused for half an hour or more at a time, simply watching for movement so that I was able to establish in which direction the creatures I was observing disappeared.

Next day I would start at the point where I had left off the day before. By altering the time and position slightly, I could follow the trail a little further until, at last, it led me to the nest I should never have stumbled on by blind luck.

It was only an extension of the theory that those who lean idly over five barred gates often see more of the sport than the huntsman chasing madly after hounds on horseback. I found that having the time to stand and watch was one of life's sweetest luxuries and I could not understand my stupidity in not having *made* time to stand and watch before. It is a marvellous feeling to be alone in deep countryside while one's friends are stifling in a writhing queue of cars, carrying them remorselessly to work for someone else.

I was able to capitalise on the regularity of habits not only to see what was about but also to notice absentees. If a waterhen was sunning herself at the same time and place for several days, the gap she left the first time she was not there was almost as conspicuous.

Closer examination might reveal a tell tale puff of feathers or bloody patch of grass which, in turn, was a clue that a stoat or fox, which I had not seen, was a fellow tenant of the wood.

The very fact that there were signs of carnage near the spot where I knew the bird spent only an hour or so each day, suggested that whatever had caught her might have passed that way in the same area of time.

In such circumstances I often found that simply going an hour earlier and hanging around, was all that was necessary to add another name to the mounting tally of acquaintances I was making.

I do not spend all my time either wandering in the wood or doing physical work there to improve it. Writing and broadcasting give me almost as much sensual pleasure as watching the things I write and broadcast about. Having once been trained in the art of Work Study, or more accurately the craft, since work studymen are crafty fellows, I am conscious that writing contains a low percentage of so-called productive work.

Out of every hour I sit at my desk, I am writing, it seems, for no more than five or ten productive minutes. The rest of the time is devoted to 'think', an element which no work study engineer can measure or rate accurately, however hard he tries and however much the Efficiency Experts try to delude their clients to the contrary. I concede that my elements of constructive thought are by no means exclusively juggling with beguiling words. My thinking would be rated highly unproductive because I find it so easy to sit for hours at my study window, simply watching whatever happens to be going on outside or day dreaming of changes which might improve the potential further.

Alarm calls of wrens or blackbirds alert me to the presence of some predator. Jays chatter differently according to whether the object of their spite is human trespasser or fox or cat; the dogs are ever watchful for the unusual.

The windows of the extension we built on are large and designed to give the illusion of sitting among the things outside instead of observing them from detachment. They succeed in this very well because everything outside has grown as accustomed to us as we are to them, so that they carry on exactly as if no stanger was about.

It was not only the wild creatures we got to know that first year. One of the joys—and sometimes trials—of living in the country is that the surrounding community is small enough to know each other personally. It follows, therefore, that a stranger settling in the district is at once an object of interest. He will not be accepted as a local for the first score of years he is there and, quite possibly, not until the next generation. But everything he does will be noted, criticised and probably exaggerated.

We live far enough off the map for it to be uneconomic for tradesfolk to make the journey especially for us and the only exception is the grocer who delivers every other week. We get no milk or bread or meat unless we go to fetch it.

There are five pubs in Abbots Bromley to pour liquid down two thousand resident throats, and most of them would be out of business if it wasn't for the trade brought by motor cars from surrounding towns.

I tried them all when we came and found the Goat's Head Inn by far the best. It is a lovely half timbered house by the Butter Cross in the centre of the village. Long and low and full of oak beams from the woods around, with winking brass and polished glass to multiply the flickering firelight a thousandfold. Tradition says that it was the Town Hall, long before it was a pub and I enjoy propping up the bar there, with my dog at my feet, listening to local gossip and tales of the past and prophesies for the future.

Twice a week I collect my milk there and am amused at strangers' expressions when I walk out with a basketful of white bottles, which we keep in the fridge till we want coffee or tea. It seems extraordinary that, even in the country, it is illegal to collect a can of 'raw' milk direct from the cowshed, warm and sweet, because of the risk of brucellosis, when generations before us seem to have drunk it with impunity.

Mabel is another anachronism. She is our postwoman and she still does her daily round of thirteen miles on a push bicycle. She arrives here about half past eleven in the morning, having left the post office about eight, and she passes us on her way home at anything up to one o'clock. Being no slave to the clock, why should she wear herself out by trying to make the sparks fly off her pedals? She is never too rushed to pass the time of day and will always stop awhile for a leisurely gossip. She is typical of the whole area. However fast the main currents flow, there are still such pleasant backwaters to cut Time down to size.

CHAPTER FIVE

The herons

The herons were the most spectacular birds in the wood and they kindled our sympathies because they had been persecuted so. Their expressive hunched grey forms breathed such dejected misery that it was impossible not to know by instinct that herons must always have had hard luck tales to tell and that ours were probably only marginally worse off than their fellows when their nesting trees in Bagot's Wood were felled, leaving their fledglings to die.

Every keeper and water bailiff and fisherman had blasted them with shot since guns made bows and arrows obsolete. Even farmers, to whom they do no harm at all, squint, beady-eyed down twelve-bore barrels if a heron crosses their land.

Add such hazards to winters like '47 and '63, when ice gave their food armour plated immunity from the sharpest bills, and it seems a miracle that any herons live at all.

That year, when the Bagot's Wood survivors first scattered their nests haphazard through Holly Covert and Dunstal Pool Plantation, they must have cursed their luck again. When the screaming saws in Lords Coppice died away, their racket was replaced by snorting caterpillar tractors dragging loads of decapitated trunks to mutilation in the saw mills.

The birds shrugged that row off because they knew that mechanical monsters like tractors and saws are not half as dangerous as a quiet man, sneaking along with a gun under his arm. But they had no means of knowing that innocent old ladies, searching for primroses or wild daffodils are one whit less lethal than louts with guns or caterpults.

However well meaning the intruder in the wood, the herons left their nests and circled high, far out of gunshot range above the trees. It was an instinct for self preservation which forbade them to return until they were convinced that the danger was so far past that safe was doubly safe.

Carrion crows are quite as slick at sliding out of harms way as the herons, though instead of circling in full view, they try to keep the solid trunks of trees between themselves and danger. The difference between them and the herons is that their cocky confidence bids them return much sooner when their threat is passed. Then they find the herons nests unguarded and eat their eggs.

It seemed marvellous that even fifteen nests survived such odds and it convinced me that any hopes of enjoying them in my wood would be short lived unless I was prepared to make some positive contribution. So far as the herons were concerned, their need was obvious. They would do no good without quiet and freedom from disturbance, especially while they were sitting on eggs or brooding vulnerable fledglings.

It was also desirable to limit the numbers of carrion crows, which were such opportunists that they were able to take instant advantage of any accidental alarm, though the herons appeared well able to take care of themselves when the crows were the only peril.

The obvious way to accomplish this was to prevent all trespass in the wood and to shoot and trap the crows. Stopping the trespass was not easy because we were not yet living here, though we did try to be on the spot at weekends and light evenings when it was worst.

The crows were even more difficult. A ferret, tethered

by a collar and line so that it can circulate in a ring of five or six yards radius is almost irresistible to crows at dawn. The moment one spots it and raises the alarm, every other crow in the wood joins in the uproar. By standing behind a tree, forty or fifty yards away, or making a straw bale hide, it was often possible to shoot five or six crows in a morning.

I used a .22 rifle, so as to make as little noise as possible and to create the minimum of disturbance. Trapping in the open is illegal, or I should have caught what I could with traps baited with eggs, for I found cage traps almost useless, though I caught plenty of jackdaws. By far the most efficient way would have been to poison them by leaving 'loaded' eggs about, but, quite apart from the fact that poison in the open is illegal, I will not use it on principle because it is so dreadfully unselective.

In the end it was poison which had finished Tough, my favourite bitch who had spent her life with me. She slept in the bedroom at night and under my desk when I was writing. When I parked my car, a lock was superfluous, for it would have been a bold man who dared to sit in my seat, and when I went out in the wood, she was always a shadow at my heels. She thundered aggressive defiance at whoever stepped within earshot and, however deserted the place may seem, I had no worries about leaving my wife alone if Tough was in the house.

I left her in the yard one day, to go out in the car, and Mabel the post woman told me she rampaged as if she would eat her when she passed a few minutes later.

When I returned in half an hour she was as cold and stiff as if she had died the day before. The post mortem showed that the cause was strychnine poisoning, which had killed my neighbour's dog the year before.

It is theoretically impossible to obtain strychnine without special permit, even by signing the poison book, and it would be illegal to lay it in the open if you did. Yet it is fairly easy to come by in Ireland and cattle dealers and travellers often bring it back undetected. They put it in eggs or dead chickens or poultry heads for foxes and crows and I imagine the poison picked up by my bitch was carried and dropped by some bird, possibly feeding its young.

It is, of course, possible that someone deliberately threw poisoned food over the fence, but knowing how the filthy stuff is commonly used, I think it more likely that it was originally laid for vermin and that my dog's death was just a careless accident.

In any case, I would rather have no herons than risk laying poison in the open for crows, though I didn't accept defeat as easily as that. I decided instead to try an experiment to persuade the herons to build their nests where I wanted them; where I could look after them when danger threatened.

The most unlikely place they could choose would be very near to human habitation, but if our herons nested close to the house, I knew they would be in less peril than in any other part of the wood. The snag was how to entice them to do so or to convince them it would be safe.

Dunstal Pool Plantation is about fourteen acres and comes up to within twenty yards of the house. It curves right round to the pool and finishes at the ride separating it from Lords Coppice and Longlands.

It so happens that it is by far the thickest and densest stand of hardwood on the place, with a canopy of oak, undergrown with hazel and birch and hawthorn and ferns. An ideal sanctuary for a wide variety of wildlife if the word sanctuary could be given bite by ridding it from disturbance.

I decided that it might encourage the herons to nest

there if nobody went into that part of the wood *including me.* I would go round its peripheral rides but would keep out of that part of the wood while the herons were there. And I would take jolly good care that nobody else went where I denied myself.

This was practicable so far as human disturbance went because, once it was accepted as desirably quiet by wild-life, any intrusion would immediately be obvious because wood pigeons would clatter out in clouds and the herons would draw my attention by spiralling above it.

On the debit side, crows would be quite as keen as any other bird on having an undisturbed sanctuary and might undo most of the good work by crowding the herons out again.

This stand of wood is a little over three hundred yards long and two hundred yards wide. None of it is beyond the sound of a rifle discharged in one of the rides around it so that I decided to see what I could do by walking round at dusk, when the crows were coming in to roost, and harassing them a little.

I waited until the pheasant shooting season was over, since I didn't want to drive my pheasants on to neigh-bours' land where they would be shot, and then I started on the crows by going round several nights a week at dusk. The first crack of my rifle knocked one off his perch and filled the whole sky with black villainy. They rose, wheel-ing dense as a pack of starlings, calling curses on my head but they couldn't locate the source of the sound.

There are always eerie echoes in the wood and if you don't actually see the flash of a rifle, it is almost impossible to pin-point it by ear. Obviously a worrying situation, if you happen to be a crow, especially if one of the flock has just thudded down to the ground for no apparent reason. I froze immobile to the trunk of my tree, waiting for the shindy to subside.

After ten minutes or so, the leaders came back and settled, all tensed-up, in the topmost branches. Another ten minutes and the rest had followed, allowing peace to reign once more. There was still a patch of sky, lit by the reflected glory of the sun, against which I could pick out the form of another old crow, so I lined the crosswire of my telescopic sight on the centre of his breast.

The crack brought him down and rekindled an encore of malediction about my ears as the whole flock rose once more into the night sky. This time they had discovered by two trials and two errors that 'my' corner of the wood was unhealthy, so they settled elsewhere, jittery as old maids in dark dockland alleys.

I repeated the performance twice nightly, though the crows soon got knowing enough never to let me shoot more than one. It didn't really matter if I shot none at all. The mere fact that a rifle cracked curfew in Dunstal Wood Plantation drove the birds up Holly Covert to the Daffodil Lawn end of the wood, where I was happy enough to leave them in peace.

By the time the herons arrived to prospect their nesting sites they found the far end of the wood seething with carrion crows, which they hate. The house end was uncannily quiet and tranquil. Not only were there no crows there but no people either. Even the grey squirrels had gone because we had spent a busy morning just after the end of the shooting season poking every squirrel drey down and shooting the occupants.

My plan worked like a dream. The first year we lived on the spot the heronry increased by almost fifty per cent, from fifteen nests to twenty-one, all but four of which were in Dunstal Pool Plantation.

We could lie in bed and hear them feeding and quarrelling and, for the few weeks between their arrival and the first clutch of eggs, there were almost continual territorial battles, whenever it was light enough to see to jab a beak. During the day they were flying ceaselessly from the heronry to Blithfield reservoir or the streams and rivers around, returning with slow flaps, scarce able to stay airborne because of their payload of fish.

After a while the crows began to infiltrate this end of the wood again because I had ceased my rifle patrols when the herons nested for fear of disturbing them again. I tried various experiments and discovered that if I let a rifle off at night by the back door, it started the crows in full voice as certainly as a conductor's baton triggers off his orchestra. The heron's didn't seem to take the slightest notice, so I fired off a few rounds haphazard into the sky to scare the crows farther up the wood without actually aiming to kill one.

The next year underlined my success by giving a tally of twenty-nine nests where young were reared successfully and in 1966 there were thirty-three. In '67 there were forty-five, '68 fifty-seven, '69 sixty-one, fifty-five of which were within a hundred yards of the house and my protection.

I plotted the increase on a graph and it was a straight enough line of gain to delight the heart of any statistician, but forces were at work to curtail the progress.

Three miles away, between the Hall and Goat Lodge, Blithfield Reservoir shimmers in the sun and scowls grey scowls when storms are in the air. It is the property of the South Staffordshire Waterworks Company Ltd who provide water for their customers and for sport. Not free sport for it is very profitable. They have stocked the reservoir with trout and charge over a hundred guineas per annum per rod for the privilege of catching them.

The fishermen naturally expect value for their hard earned brass so the water works company keeps a chain of tanks for rearing trout to restock the water.

Our herons were not welcomed with open arms in competition with fee paying guests and some of them were shot. Because herons are such persecuted birds, subject to being shot and disturbed while breeding, poisoned from eating frogs, dying from agricultural pesticides, and starved in hard winters, they have been placed on the schedule of protected birds.

Although the herons were unaware of this symbol of their status, it was an astute political move, calculated to gather a few votes from dedicated bird lovers without losing votes from anglers who probably outnumber ornithologists by ten to one.

The reason it didn't offend the sportsmen was that the wily bureaucrats left a line in their protection bill saying it was illegal to kill herons *unless* they could be proved to be doing damage to a fishery.

As it is presumably damaging to have expensively reared fish killed by anything but rod and line, even a respectable body like the South Staffordshire Waterworks Company was not blotting its copybook too badly by shooting these predatory birds on its fishery.

Luckily for me the resident engineer in charge of Blithfield reservoir, R. W. Robertson is a helpful chap who, though he probably regards my behaviour as eccentric, can see that I have taken positive steps to help what is undoubtedly a bird under great pressure. When I complained about his water bailiff shooting 'my' herons, he sent me a couple of thousand perch 'to keep my hungry brutes at home'.

He admitted that one of the worst menaces to his fishery is the quantity of coarse fish which breed there and compete with trout for food as well as feeding on young trout small enough for other fish to eat.

Every year the bailiff anchors cage traps for perch which catch them on roughly the same principle as lobsters in a lobster pot. Most of these perch are sold to coarse fishermen to stock canals, where they sit in rows on crates of beer, fishing the water with maggots on hooks.

It started a train of thought which set me wondering if herons are the menace they are supposed to be, certainly to trout. Our herons come to nest in February and disperse when the last broods are fledged in late August or September. The time they are here in greatest concentration is spring when the coarse fish are spawning. This is also the period of most rapid growth of their young, so that they take the greatest volume of food at this time.

Examination of the undigested food pellets they eject beneath the nests confirmed that most of the food the young were eating contained the scales and bones of perch not trout. There were also masses of the remains of frogs and toads and few water voles and moles.

So the evidence suggested that during the spring and summer the herons were doing the trout more good than harm by killing competitive and predatory fish.

At the turn of the year, when trout are spawning and therefore vulnerable in the shallows, the herons are dispersed at anything up to a hundred miles radius, so there aren't enough concentrated here to wreak material carnage.

When I put this to Rob, he said that, as the graph of the number of heron nests had climbed, the number of perch caught in his traps had decreased. There may, of course be no connection between the two results, but I believe that it is more than possible that the herons here may well have done positive good to the game fish in the reservoir by an effective cull of their fishy enemies.

Catching trout at the fish tanks is quite another matter. Great, idle hand-fed fish loll around the surface of these tanks, sitting targets for any herons which perch on the sides.

In 1970, 'our' nests declined from sixty-one the year

before to fifty-five, and I gather that nineteen birds—protected birds the politicians would have us believe—were caught in the act of robbing the fish tanks and executed. Otherwise it seems likely that the increase in numbers would have been maintained to give a total of around seventy nests.

One hopeful sign is that it now seems that the worst predation at the tanks is not the work of birds but men. The tanks are so isolated that tempting but untraceable fish have appeared on fishmonger's slabs which may not have died a sporting death.

To cut this risk, they are erecting a security net round the whole area and I hope a guard dog will take charge. It would need so little training to encourage him to 'see off' such large birds with as much enthusiasm as taking the pants off a poacher. Failing that, Rob is considering roofing the enclosure with netting to keep the herons out entirely.

The herons provide us with all sorts of amusement as well as the challenge of helping them to increase their numbers. After the tankful of coarse fish from the reservoir was emptied in our pool, the banks looked like the river Severn when the Birmingham anglers are having a bonanza. I counted over thirty grey forms lining the edge of the pool, hunched and dejected, but with keen competitive eyes focused to harpoon the first fish that strayed within striking distance.

It was tremendous fun to watch them through binoculars, because it then became obvious that their statuesque stance was no more than a pose. They were poised to make jabs which would leave lightning at the starting post and the fish which I saw caught never knew what hit them.

One day, when I was walking in the wood with a naturalist friend, we came across great gobs of gelatinous mucus about the size of egg yolks. It was what the ancients knew as star rot or star slime, the rot of the stars. They thought it was all that was left when a shooting star hit earth and some credence was lent to the theory by the fact that blobs of this star rot have been found in the complete isolation of places like Dartmoor as well as on farmland and in woods.

The real explanation is more prosaic, for the slime we found had almost certainly been left by herons, and it is part of the gelatinous glands in the oviducts of frogs and toads.

Anyone who has watched a frog spawning will have marvelled at the immense volume of spawn so tiny an animal is capable of producing. The fact is that the frog could not contain such a spectacular volume at all. It is only when the tiny eggs are laid that they attract water and swell into the masses of spawn which float in springtime pools and puddles.

If a bird ate a frog before it spawned and its digestive juices made the eggs swell on anything like that sort of scale, it is obvious that it would be extremely uncomfortable if not fatal. So herons, and probably other birds, such as crows, do not eat the oviducts of the frogs and toads they catch. They disembowel them and leave the oviducts untouched. When they are exposed to the moisture in the atmosphere or rain or dew, the glands swell up to leave the lumps of jelly which our forefathers thought had dropped from the stars.

When the herons first arrive to nest, they spend many hours on the ground within sight of the heronry. The place ours choose is in a forty acre field opposite the dining-room window.

Later in the season, when they are not away fishing, they perch on or near their nests, but they always begin on this gathering ground, hunched and dejected as ever, completely ignoring each other. Sometimes, when a newcomer arrives, he does not simply flop down but flies in with uncharacteristic gaiety and skips along the edge of the group. This extrovert behaviour stimulates the other birds out of their normal lethargy and they join in to give a few hops and skips of dance before relapsing to attitudes of utter indifference.

Nobody could describe it as a sexy courtship dance, for the birds exhibit no more enthusiasm than deadpan modern youths, jigging idly up and down to pop groups, out of all physical contact with their partners.

They are birds which take all their pleasures sadly. When the stiff formality of their courtship is done, more as a duty than as a delight, they get down to the chores of building their nests, though nobody would accuse them of being houseproud even here. They sit miserably over them, apparently getting more physical pleasure from quarrelling with their neighbours than lovemaking with their mates.

CHAPTER SIX

In ages past

In these times of insecurity, when values have slipped and no man can predict what lies ahead, it is comforting to be thrown into close contact with the past.

There are seven goats heads over the porch of our house, superbly carved in local stone. Every crinkle of their curving horns is cut into eternity and their beards, which merge with the dressed stone blocks above the front door, will still be there when we are dust. The Bagot Coat of Arms is carved beneath the overhanging oak gable and the goat's head crest proudly proclaims that this was once part of the Bagot estate which encompassed many thousand acres.

The house itself is dressed stone at the base with cladding above of thick oak planks, pegged into the overlaps with stout oak pegs. The roof is not slate or tiles but wooden shingles, originally of oak, though the more recent ones on the part we have added are made of cedar.

Towering above the roof is a massive oak chimney, surmounted by deers' heads, also carved in stone, with stone arrows pointing down towards the house. The gracious hall window is glazed with tiny panes, held not as leaded lights but in an intricate frame of cast iron, and there is a bow and two quivers of arrows carved in stone above it.

Even when it was built, in about 1835, it must have cost a mint. It was conceived and designed by Buckler, who made additions and alterations to Blithfield Hall at about the same time and it is typical of an era when folk had enough faith in the future to build as well as they could with materials of the highest quality. Each of the dressed stones weighs several hundredweights and, when we drilled through the walls to put air bricks to ventilate the floors, we cut through twenty-one solid inches before we saw daylight again.

Despite such craftsmanship, it was really a 'folly' in the sense that it was built more for its external appearance than for comforts within. The hall window is the right proportions for the gable exterior, but not for the hall itself, for the top of the window pokes up into the bedroom above.

The oak planks are not really pegged as they seem to be. They are bolted into a solid brick wall beneath them and the bolt heads are simply capped by oak pegs disguised as genuine dowels, to hide the bolts.

The vital statistics of the house are designed to display its external shell, but that did not mean that charms concealed from casual callers were any the less alluring. The class of the place is such that we found it as dry as a chip when we arrived although it had stood empty for two years.

I cock a snook at my past by calling the row of carved goats heads my Board of Directors, though they make less stupid decisions than I did, and I rate their inscrutable wisdom higher than human pomposity. They are symbollic of permanence almost undreamed of in these times of shifty values.

The Goat's Head Inn, Goat Lodge and the goat's head on the Bagot crest are all connected through the centuries to the Bagot family. In the times of the crusaders, the only ways of getting fresh meat or fresh milk when armies were at war was either to pillage it or to take it with you. And the only way to take it with you, but still have it fresh

Miss Roedoe comes to study window for biscuits at coffee time

Goat Lodge from ride opposite house

Duck on Dunstal Pool ice

A stag-headed oak that was there 1,000 years before Goat Lodge

Fetching the logs for winter. Author, Spider, Tough (tailend), Fly and Mandy (lurchers)

The naturalist's perfect companion. Tick, the German short-haired pointer bitch

Collared doves and ptarmigan pigeons at bird table by window

Lady Bagot and her daughter Cara feeding the Bagot goats

Bagot goats and kids in Holly Covert

The Bagot goats on Daffodil Lawn

Heron sunning itself by Dunstal Pool

The heronry in Dunstal Pool Plantation

Heron fishing in Dunstal Pool

when you wanted it, was to drive it on the hoof or to keep it alive on board ship.

Domestic cattle and sheep were not well suited to such a nomadic life, particularly when forced marches were necessary. Apparently goats were better and tradition has it that the crusaders brought some of their goats home from the wars with them. Their bodies were white and their heads and necks were black, like the Schwarzhals, or black necked goats of the Rhone valley, so that their ancestors probably came from that district.

The original herd of goats were presented to Sir John Bagot by King Richard II, in appreciation of the hunting he had enjoyed in Bagot's Park, and the goats head on the Bagot crest dates from the time of King Richard II.

There is a wonderful sense of tranquillity in being integrated with an estate with such continuous associations with the past and roots which dig so deep. Many superstitions grow out of such antiquity and some say that if the goats die out the Bagots would go. They have roamed the Bagot estates for the six centuries since Sir John Bagot's day and, by the beginning of the last war, the herd was several hundred strong. Almost a thousand acres of Bagot's Park was enclosed by an oak paling deer fence, but its confines were mostly feggy grass and bracken and rush.

The desperate wartime shortage of food forced the authorities to order part of it, where the oaks were not too thick, to be ploughed and reseeded and the more intractable part to be used as a bombing range. The goats, they said, must go.

But the goats were part of the England men were fighting for; certainly part of this bit of England. So some were reprieved and allowed to run in Bagot's Wood, which was about a thousand acres of ancient hardwood, which provided ideal feeding.

By this time the estate had already begun to suffer the

erosion of taxation, which has ruined and split up the lands of so many famous English families. Just before the war, land had been commandeered for Blithfield Reservoir, though the valley of the Blythe was not actually flooded until after the war. The Fifth Lord Bagot, who owned it, had sold the hall with it, though it was agreed that he could continue to live there for the rest of his days.

After the war, in 1946, he died and was succeeded by his cousin, the Sixth Lord, whose wife Nancy, was an Australian. Their first task was to dispose of the remaining contents of the hall which had to be turned over to the South Staffordshire Waterworks Company within six months of the fifth Lord's death. They stayed at a pub in Abbots Bromley and walked over to Blithfield every day, growing more reluctant with each visit to be the first Bagots not to live there.

The result was inevitable. Despite the dereliction and ruinous state of the house and garden, they fell so in love with it that they breathed life into the old place once more.

It was a pretty daunting task. There was no electricity and only one stark tap in the basement of the house, from which every drop of water had to be carried to hip baths and basins in the bedrooms. There was no sanitation or central heating and rain poured through the roof. The gardens were a jungle and the central courtyard was used as a fowl pen because it was the one place safe from foxes.

The kitchen wing was crumbling with dry rot and had to be pulled down but by the time Caryl the sixth lord died, in 1961, he and his wife had re-created not just a stately home but a homely one. Nancy Lady Bagot, his wife, has devoted the rest of her life to continuing the restoration which will live on when most of us have been forgotten.

She still owns the hall and grounds, but the rest of the estate was split up and sold by the next heir, and when we came to Goat Lodge, there was still a couple of thousand acres of the estate for sale. This included Bagot's Wood, which had been felled and let to the Forestry Commission for replanting, Bagot's Park and several farms and cottages.

The Forestry Commission were understandably not anxious to have the goats among their young plantations, so the ones Lady Bagot had not taken up to the Hall before the sale, were driven into the park. When the new heir sold out, the goats were put up as a separate lot.

Putting them up for sale and selling them were quite different. Every man's hand had been against them ever since the war and farmers had even fired on them with shotguns if they trespassed. The only reason they had survived was that they had reverted to the wild and, when I first knew them, it was easier to approach a wild deer than a Bagot's goat.

Most of the herd were eventually driven into a stockade and sold, the majority fortunately to a Bagot kinsman, but about a dozen escaped back to their old haunts.

Brian Dale, the new owner of the park intended to reclaim the land for farming, so he didn't want them there and the Forestry Commission had not chalked up welcome on their young trees. Our wood was their only other possible refuge.

Dunstal Pool Plantation is the densest part of the whole wood, but there are only two miserable hollies left in Holly Covert, though a book that Lady Bagot lent me describes 'forest sized' holly trees there last century. There is no doubt what has happened to those hollies in the meantime. The goats have eaten them or ringbarked them until they have died.

Goats love broadleaved plants, honeysuckle and bramble and sycamore and oak, and they adore succulent bark like holly. When there is any concentration of goats, they nip off all young shoots and inhibit all regeneration. This is all too easy to see if you stand in the ride between Dunstal Pool Plantation and Holly Covert. The covert is such open woodland that it is possible to see a pheasant run a hundred yards away. He would never run that far in the pool plantation because the undergrowth is thick enough for him to skulk and hide.

The reason for this is that, when the trees in Bagot's Wood were felled the Forestry Commission fenced in their young plantation, leaving a smaller area for the goats to wander over without getting on to farmland.

Such a herd can soon wreak expensive damage to a crop of standing corn, so Lord Bagot put a fence from the forestry boundary right across to the east side of Longlands, which excluded them from the pool plantation and the farmland to the south.

Seeing the trail of havoc they left, I was none too keen to have them in my wood. It would be practically impossible to improve the quality and variety if they were there to nip everything I planted in the bud. Bagot goats had been here for six centuries while I had scarce been here six months. They had more right to the woods than I had and, if I had kicked them out, I should have severed a link with the past which I could never forge again. I may know who my grandfather was, but I cannot trace my lineage much further. The ancestors of the goats were here, in the same spot, before my grandfather's grandfather's grandfather saw the light of day.

At about this time, the goats which Lady Bagot had taken to the Hall were going through a sticky patch and dying off faster than they bred. The reason was that, like sheep, goats are infested with internal parasites which are expelled with their dung and can be reingested at another stage in their life cycle as goats graze the pasture.

Being browsing animals, this does not happen much in the wild because they grab a tasty mouthful, move on and do not return that way till any parasites they passed have perished.

Lady Bagot had been forced to confine them in a relatively small enclosure of a few acres, and it did not take this pasture long to get 'goat sick', so that they kept re-infecting themselves and building up cumulative internal troubles.

The goats in our wood were escapees from the sale and I felt that their rightful place was with the rest of the herd at the Hall, but suggested a compromise which might be of mutual benefit.

I would send the goats from here to join their kin when they were on view to the public when the house opened in the spring. This would rest the ground here and allow us to get a crop of hay to feed them in winter off Daffodil Lawn, which had been used to grow hay for the goats for generations.

Then, when the Hall was closed to the public in the autumn, the whole herd could come back here, giving the Blithfield pasture a chance to recover and get sweet again.

These woods are well sheltered and there is a warm goat shed to attract them away from vulnerable farm land. This has worked quite well and the once wild creatures, chivvied and shot whenever they dared poke a horn from cover, are now tame enough to feed from strangers' hands. They are at last confident that nobody wishes them ill.

They spend the winter here and choose the most inconvenient times to produce their kids, which always seem to arrive in deep snow or blizzard or when rain as cold as ice is bucketing down, so I feed them with hay and sheep nuts to try to keep them near their shed.

The nannies still sneak off to some solitary accouchement bed of bracken and leave their kids, lying lonely as fallow fawns, returning only to suckle them.

If the weather is harsh enough to weaken them, the foxes sometimes take them the moment the mother goes off to feed. So I creep round in all weathers, rescuing the vulnerable ones and putting them in the goat shed out of danger's way.

Mary Jackson did the job before me and her father before her. It is one of the delightful chores I inherited with Goat Lodge and I get deep satisfaction in being a link in this chain which binds the past to the present.

Arriving at the moment of disintegration of the estate meant that it was a period of greater change than these parts have seen for centuries. Bagot's Park itself was an extraordinary place. About a couple of hundred yards over the boundary of Daffodil Lawn the skyline is dominated by Lord Bagot's Walking Stick. This is an oak tree which must be unique. Instead of being stout and gnarled, it has a trunk as straight as a telegraph pole which is seventy-five feet to the first branch.

In theory it is likely to have had other trees around it to draw it to such a height, but there are no other trees as tall anywhere in the area. I have discussed this with lots of people skilled in forestry, but all have been equally baffled.

Mary Jackson's cousin gave me a picture postcard of the Walking Stick Oak, with her father, who was woodman, on one side and Mary's father, who was keeper and goatherd, on the other. The picture was taken over sixty years ago and they were discussing whether it ought to be felled because it had just been struck by lightning.

I have another picture, taken fifty-five years later, with Lady Bagot on one side and her daughter Cara on the other. The tree looks little the worse for the interval and the discussion this time was not whether it should be felled but how we were to prevent it.

Before Brian Dale could recoup his cash by reclaiming the park as a farm, it was necessary to drain and plough the sour land and, before this could be done, there were hundreds of trees to be moved. They were mostly oak trees of great age, some perhaps a thousand years old and most of them 'stag-headed'. That is to say that the branches at the top of the tree were dying and carried no foliage, even in high summer.

The local woodmen said they were 'shook'—or shaken. When they were cut down, some had radial cracks from the centre of the trunk to the bark. The woodmen said these had been standing in too much water, which had been drawn up and split the trunk. That was 'star shake'.

Others had circular cracks and were said to be 'ring shook', the cause being attributed to the tree growing lop-sided so that the winds of centuries had tried to rotate it like a horizonal windmill. The theories probably hold no more water than the cracks in the trunks, but I never write off such country beliefs as rubbish because so many of them are subsequently proved to have something in them.

When the fourth Lord died in 1932, there had been a tremendous felling of Bagot oaks to meet taxation, and it was said that ten thousand of the finest trees in England crashed to the ground for a mere ten thousand pounds.

The stag headed ones which were left when we came were mostly the remnants which were not of sufficient commerical value to bother about thirty years before. So clearing out these old trees to make way for the plough was not the tragedy to strangers that it might seem to locals who are naturally resistant to change.

There were however a few which it seemed a crime to despoil. Lord Bagot's Walking Stick was one, so I used the picture of Lady Bagot and her daughter standing by it as illustration for a weekly column I write for the Birmingham *Evening Mail,* in which I pleaded for its life.

Brian Dale relented with the Walking Stick but the other famous oaks have died or been grubbed out. Five of them were so important that they were marked individually on the ordnance map. They were the Squitch Oak, the Venison Oak, the King's Oak and the Queen's Oak, though I do not know which king and which queen were so honoured.

Most famous of all was the Beggar's Oak. Its shadow covered a quarter of an acre. In olden days the Bagots thought so much of their oaks that, if a branch cracked, it was sawn off to sound wood near the trunk and the cut end was plated with lead sheet to keep the weather out. Quite a standard for us who follow to live up to.

Besides being plated where it had been damaged, the Beggar's Oak had all its main branches propped with struts because each was as large as a normal tree and in danger of shattering under its own great weight or tearing away from the trunk, which was hollow.

It had apparently been hollow for centuries because the legend was that once, when a previous owner was riding in the park, a beggar asked for alms and was refused. He crept, dispirited into the hollow tree to die from exposure but, before he died, he cursed the Bagots, saying that they would never sire another son to inherit their estate and that, when the Beggar's Oak fell down, it would be the end of their reign.

He was wrong about the son because the estate did pass to direct male heirs until the fourth lord died in 1932. This was the time when ten thousand oaks were felled, after which the estate passed from cousin to cousin till Caryl, the sixth Lord died in 1961.

The estate was then broken up and sold and the Beggar's Oak collapsed.

The drive to Goat Lodge goes on past Holly Covert

and leaves our land to cross the Park, running on two miles more before it joins a public road again at the top of Buttermilk hill. As wild a bit of country as it is possible to imagine in the Midlands, and Park Lodge, the farm at the far end of the park lends colour to any dreams you care to dream.

It is a large straggling house looking out on to what was once open parkland but is now only a prairie of plough. The group of buildings one field away at the back was originally built for a pack of hounds.

These were no common foxhounds. They were the pack of bloodhounds for which the Bagots were famous. Park Lodge was not always a simple farm either. It has panelled rooms downstairs and far more bedrooms than an ordinary farmhouse would need.

The story is that it was once a hunting lodge and that the bloodhounds were ostensibly kept for tracking down wounded deer in the woods. They were no encouragement to poachers but they also had a far more offbeat use.

A century and a half ago, the family always threw a Christmas party at Blithfield which would put our effete modern parties in the shade. It lasted for the whole fortnight over Christmas and, on Boxing day, the cooks and servants were sent over from Blithfield at dawn to prepare luncheon at Park Lodge.

They were followed after breakfast by the male members of the party, who enjoyed a day's shooting, and the ladies rode over in carriages in time for lunch. This is recalled in a novel by a contemporary Bagot, and there is a lovely description of the ride through Holly Covert, which was under a blanket of snow, that accentuated the beauty of the 'forest sized' holly trees.

On New Year's Eve there was a ball at the hall to which the local tradesmen and doctors and senior servants of the family were invited.

On the stroke of midnight the doors of the ballroom were thrown open and the pack of Bagot bloodhounds screamed through the guests in full cry. The book doesn't say who laid the trail or whether they pulled down their quarry up on the archery ground or deep in Blithfield Grove. But whether they regarded it as a dramatic end of the old year or a spine chilling burst of hound music to herald in the New, no guest there would ever forget it.

We had just absorbed enough of the atmosphere of the place to feel at peace with its solitude and in tune with its traditions when we got a shock.

John Lewis, who was creating the fertile farm in the park for the new owner, turned up one day with a lump of baked clay covered with cracked glaze. He said he had found it in the park when they had been bulldozing out the roots of some of the ancient trees.

I was in no doubt about its origin because I had seen so many similar lumps in the Stourbridge area of the Black Country. It was part of a clay crucible used for melting glass and the cracked glaze adhering to one surface was the glass skin which had welded to it when it had cooled.

The mystery was how it had got into Bagot's Park? When we searched the spot where it had been found, we soon found plenty more. There were bits of crucible, gobs of glass which had been poured out and left to set solid, thin broken glass and ancient hand made bricks. These were thinner and less even in size than modern bricks, spewed out identical from mass producing moulds.

Our first theory was that somebody had dumped a few loads of rubbish from a local glass works. But the nearest glass works we could think of was a dozen miles away at Tutbury, and it would surely have been uneconomic to bring heavy waste so far, especially as there wasn't a hard road within a mile.

I called in Robert Sherlock, the Industrial Archaeologist attached to Staffordshire County Council, and he was agog with interest. He sent samples to the Victoria and Albert museum, who proclaimed that they were medieval glass. Searching among old Bagot papers, he discovered an agreement between Richard Bagot and Ambrose Henesy Gent, with Thomas Tysoc as one of the witnesses.

This agreement, made in June 1585, stipulated that Richard Bagot should erect a glasshouse in Bagot's Park and supply wood at the glasshouse door for two and four pence a cord.

Tysoc was to provide ashes and clay and other necessaries for making glass and to repay a loan of £40, presumably for working capital, to Richard Bagot within a year either in cash or in finished glass.

Richard Bagot had to supply lodgings for the glassmakers and it seems they were to split the profits.

The enterprise flourished for thirty years and petered out through royal decree not inefficiency. So much English oak was being felled all over the country to make iron and glass that there was a real danger of running out of the raw materials to build the warships so vital to our safety.

The King issued a decree forbidding the felling of timber for furnaces and a pathetic letter from Walter Bagot in 1615 begs permission to continue to use his own wood to make glass in his own park.

He was apparently unsuccessful for about the same time there are records of a Tysoc and a Henesy starting the glass trade in the Stourbridge area of the Black Country.

As John Lewis continued to clear the park to make way for the plough he uncovered the remains of many more furnaces. There seems to have been one about every four hundred yards, though they probably followed each other and were not all there at once.

The reason for starting glass works at the back of beyond

was because transport was a major difficulty. It was easier to build a furnace near its source of fuel, and to cart away the relatively small volume of finished glass, than to carry bulky tree trunks over the rough tracks that served as roads.

The life of the furnace was limited because it eventually burnt out and had to be rebuilt so that the obvious thing was not to rebuild it on its old site but to move the new one over nearer to the untapped source of fuel, to reduce the carriage of wood to the glasshouse door.

Little was known about the technicalities of flues or the detailed design of the furnaces of those days, so a professional archaeologist was sent from Sheffield University to investigate. He brought a team of students to dig out a furnace near the banks of the Story Brook, near the centre of the park. Unfortunately he failed to excavate a site marked by a circular track on the hill above which was thought to have been a horse operated grinding mill, possibly to grind scrap glass or cullet for the mixture to be melted in the furnace.

The glass which the Bagots and their partners made here seems to have been window glass. This wasn't rolled flat, as it is by modern practice, but blown in cylinders, having a large diameter and a very short length, like round biscuits.

When this cooled, the edges were cut off leaving the ends of the cylinder as two flat plates, which could then be cut into panes of any size or shape.

There was a thick blob in the centre of these cylinders where they had been attached to the blowing iron. This was the blob in the centre of old 'bottle' windows and would only have been used on cheap dwellings because it was regarded as scrap. Now it is fashionable to make panes deliberately to look like this to give olde worlde shoppes and houses a false air of antiquity.

Being wise after the event it should have caused us no surprise that there had once been a thriving glass trade here. The local ordnance map is plastered with names such as Glass Bank and Glass Lane and Glasshouse Farm.

King James, who stopped it, is now my favourite monarch. If he had not applied the pressures which sent Tysoc and Henesy to King's Swinford near Stourbridge, our wood might have gone and the air might now echo to thudding drop hammers instead of harmless herons.

CHAPTER SEVEN

The hunters

There is room in the countryside for all sorts of people but I confess to wishing some of them anywhere but here. We are plagued by strangers who expect me to disturb my 'pretty' badgers from their diurnal rest because they are too idle or ignorant to give themselves the thrill of watching wild badgers going about their crepuscular business. Fond mums try to deluge us with their spoilt brats who they wish to photograph against a backcloth of roe deer, and tail waggers think our wood ideal for exercising their pets because there are so many scents to thrill a doggy nose and so much exciting furry quarry for them to chase. I have not the least compunction about showing them all the door.

A party of orienteers turned up one day and seemed hurt that I had no idea what orienteering was and angry that I wouldn't let them go into the wood when they had explained its meaning.

They get their fun, it seems, with maps and enjoy setting off from one obscure map reference with the object of reaching another without getting lost. A gaggle of them wanted to charge through our wood on individual courses, choosing what each calculated would be the quickest route with map and compass, the man arriving at the predetermined finish first being adjudged the winner.

It was obvious that they would have disturbed more in half an hour than I do in a year, trampling wild flowers, flushing birds from their nests and driving the pheasants and deer over my boundaries.

I put my point but they were not impressed. They had no interest in pheasants, except on a plate; they thought of wild flowers as weeds and that the countryside was for the free enjoyment of all.

I could see but one argument in reply. At risk of bruising their well padded sensitivity, I told them that I had worked hard all my life and dissipated the savings on a place with no public access especially to avoid the likes of them. We had nothing in common and I invited them to leave before I put them off by force.

Shooting men are at the other end of my scale. I rarely shoot, except at vermin with a rifle or an odd pheasant for the pot, for my marksmanship is such that I could scarcely hit a bull in an entry. That does not mean that I want to stop all better shots from having sport with pheasants.

If they enjoy seeing birds crumple in a puff of feathers, that is their affair, not mine. I am only concerned that they should not endanger species already beset by the spectre of rarity or preserve their pheasants to the peril of all else. I can understand that such people resent the dedicated do-gooders who presume to tell them that it is amoral to go hunting or shooting or fishing because it does not meet with their approval. Such bigoted cranks do their cause more harm than good.

Brian Dale, my neighbour told me that, since he lives some miles away, he was going to allow a syndicate to shoot over his land here but that I could still go where I like with my dogs.

He is a very good neighbour so that I was naturally anxious to be co-operative when one of the syndicate called to see if he 'and a few friends' could have the last drive in my wood when they were shooting on the adjoining estate.

Bagot's Wood, having been entirely replanted, is

short of natural feed and I knew that a good many of the birds they reared would drift into Holly Covert to feed on the bilberries and blackberries and acorns when they were ripe, so I agreed provided they only shot pheasants.

I never knew a man could have so many friends. I had been brought up among sportsmen who regarded about six guns as the maximum number so I was somewhat taken aback when a troupe of about thirty arrived.

They seemed to be mostly farmers whose boyish sense of fun belied their years. Their virile mirth gave plenty of warning of their approach, but if no quarry stirred, no one seemed to mind. One fellow caused uproar by flinging his neighbour's hat on high and shooting a hole through it in midair and they had a sweepstake on the size of the bag.

When they did get down to business, they were ruthlessly efficient. They covered the whole of our wood in about two great swaths, mowing down all before them like locusts eating blades of corn. I noticed that it was only the sinews of his great age which held one old cock together for a young bird would have been blown to pieces by such devastating fire power.

They passed on and the last I saw of them was a line of silhouettes moving as soldiers over the skyline of Squitch Bank, reminding me that sport is war without its risks.

It was an example of the different outlooks which must somehow shake down together in the countryside. They hate owls and foxes and stoats and weasels because they might compete with them for pheasants.

I admire a pheasant's beauty and would go to as great lengths to conserve him as I would for a kingfisher—if pheasants were as rare. But since they are common and as easily reared as domestic fowl, it goes against my grain to put other things at risk on their behalf.

The shooters caused as much disturbance as the orienteers would have done but it was far easier to make them see sense because they could see both sides through rural eyes.

They didn't ask to come again and I believe that they spare the hawks and owls and badgers on their beat, not because it would be illegal to do otherwise but because they appreciate that we have far more in common than would appear on the surface.

I reciprocate by taking only enough cock pheasants for the pot and I never harm a hen. I feed the rides around the house because I enjoy the sight of pheasants and deer and small birds in fearless profusion, so that the wood acts as a reservoir where the pheasants stay to breed wild instead of straying on to more perilous places. In autumn they spill back into the kale which sprouts as if by magic just over my boundary. This echoes with an annual fusillade so that I know, and I know that the shooters know that I know, that they would have less pheasants and I would have less hawks and owls without this mutual co-operation.

I have also had minor differences of opinion with the local hunt. My attitude to hunting is the same as to shooting. I would do all in my power to prevent men killing otters with hounds or traps or poison or by destroying their habitat. It makes no difference to me, and precious little to the otter, if he is killed accidentally by pesticides or for fun with hounds.

My protective instinct is aroused because the otter is a threatened species, whose breeding holes are destroyed by clearing river banks of roots for better drainage, whose privacy is destroyed by weekly lines of fishermen and whose diet is poisoned by agricultural chemicals. Unless somebody does something positive to help otters they will grow rare to the point of extinction.

By the same token, I would rather see partridges on the

schedule of protected birds than in some trigger-happy Harry's gamebag. Changing methods of farming have removed hedgerows where partridge love to nest and the fashion of ploughing stubble as soon as the corn is harvested has limited their chances of gleaning grain right through the winter and has cut their numbers down.

Chemical pesticides have almost exterminated some of the insects that are vital if partridge chicks are to survive the first few weeks of life and a succession of late cold springs have added insult to their injuries.

So I am against hunting otters or shooting partridges, not because other people enjoy such sport more than I do but for the practical reason that both species need help not harassment.

So far as I am concerned, foxhunting comes into the same bracket as shooting and orienteering. They all disturb things quite unconnected with the objects of their sport, and foxhunters and orienteers seem to expect to rush over the countryside wherever they like, though shooting men at least rent the rights and keep off land where the owner does not wish to strike a bargain.

The first brush I had with the foxhunting fraternity was easy to deal with. A local hunt, the boundary of whose country ended more than a mile from us, hunted their fox across the road into Bagot's Wood. (Hunts decide their territory by agreement with other hunts more than by agreement with landowners.)

When they got to our wood, the hounds decided that deer smelt sweeter than foxes, and possibly that they didn't bite so hard. So they split into two or three groups, all hunting different deer.

The first I knew about it was when our own dogs rousled out of sleep and rushed barking to the window and, there to my horror, were a group of foxhounds trying to get through the fence to my tame roe deer.

The netting round the house, pool and paddock is six feet high, which seemed reasonably safe to keep the hounds out. The greatest danger was that they would so terrify the deer that they would rush in mad panic headlong into the farthest netting from the hounds.

If this happened to be close to a support post it might break the deer's neck or legs, but there was a more insidious hazard. If a deer collided with the netting full tilt, with neck outstretched, a horizontal wire could easily damage or extract her teeth. This might have the same effect that I have seen in old sheep, whose teeth had decayed with age. They could no longer crop the grass and grew thinner and thinner until they died of slow starvation.

The hunt had given no warning of their coming, but I was soon outside, warning them to go. The huntsman tootled on his horn till he grew red in the face, but his hounds took not the slightest notice. So I explained my fears in plainer language and was firm about the fact that I should be glad to see the back of him.

He said his hounds were 'only' hunting fallow deer and seemed as incapable of knowing or caring about the side effects on my roe deer as the orienteers about nesting birds. In any case, they were my fallow deer he was hunting without permission since deer are presumed, in law, to belong to the owner of the land where they are at the moment.

Seeing the futility of reason, I fetched a rifle, ostentatiously poked a bullet up the spout, and calmly told him that I would shoot the first hound that scaled the netting.

That was something he understood. He dug his heels into his nag and disappeared for safety in a camouflaging cloud of mud.

I could hear him hollering his hounds in the distance, probably from behind some tree where he thought he was out of range! A couple of younger, bolder members of the hunt came galloping round, whipped off the hounds and departed with my maledictions still ringing in their ears.

Threatening hounds with a gun is a worse offence in the country than belching at table in polite society. I imagined that, if I had been rated eccentric before, I might well be beyond the pale now but it caused me no undue worry.

Two or three years later the hunt in question folded-up and was engulfed by the Meynell. This is a very different pack, which has always been held in high esteem by sporting folk and is hunted by Dermot Kelly, a master with a reputation for being an artist at his job.

He lost no time in putting me at a disadvantage. Instead of allowing his hounds to rampage unannounced over the place, risking the fate of such uninvited guests, he turned up one afternoon to introduce himself.

He said he would be hunting in the area next season and had I any objection if his hounds came into the wood?

Having spent a lifetime with working dogs, I know perfectly well that if his hounds were hunting a fox which took refuge here, or even crossed the land, there would be precious little he could do about it. And, as I said, there is room in the country for all sorts of people.

Having been spiked on the end of a polite request which it might be churlish to refuse, I deemed it fair enough to reply in kind. So I innocently asked if his hounds were steady to deer.

He had to admit, of course, that they might riot on a deer 'if it happened to run across their path', but what hounds would not?

I pointed out that my dogs are all steady and that we have a nice lot of fallow deer which do nobody any harm —so long as they are here. But if they are scattered by trespassers, foxhounds or other intruders, they stray on to farm land where they are liable to be shot.

I showed him my badger setts, my tame roe deer and our conversation rattled on in mutual interest for a couple of hours or so. By the time he went, we had hacked out a sensible compromise. I said that I wouldn't grumble if he hunted a fox through the wood and he agreed to move them out as quickly as he could and certainly not allow them to draw the cover, driving all before them as they combed the undergrowth.

Three weeks later they were cubhunting three miles away and the pack split, some hounds following a fox into Bagot's Wood. The first I knew was the sight of deer going in all directions and I heard the cry of hounds right up in Lord's Coppice. I heaved a few stones at them but couldn't get near enough to convince them I was in no mood for pleasantries. So I jumped in the car and asked Dermot Kelly to come and get them out.

He didn't come for three hours, so I took the law into my own hands, caught the three remaining hounds and shut them in an outhouse. When he finished hunting, he noticed he was a couple and a half short and came over here to look for them. He couldn't believe they had let me catch them, but I told him I'd picked them up exhausted when my deer had run them to a standstill. He wasn't fooled by that, but I only admitted to putting salt on their tails, and he never discovered how I caught them.

Catching-up hounds while they are hunting is considered almost as eccentric in the country as threatening them with a gun, but we didn't fall out in spite of that.

I don't really think they do all that much damage and I love to see any dog work, from a sheep dog to a fox-hound. Any top class huntsman needs more than a working knowledge of natural history and I knew that he could see as easily as the shooters that the less disturbance he caused here the better my chances of success. So we parted with mutual respect and he paid me the compliment, at the end of the season, of inviting me to propose the toast of Foxhunting at his Hunt Supporters supper.

I am not so incurably crusty that my face would crack if a smile of welcome crossed it. One of the joys of working so closely with wildlife is the number of friends I meet with similar interests, and among the most welcome of our guests are the senior girls of the School of St Mary and St Anne.

It was some years since I had first met the staff and offered facilities for the few girls actively interested in Natural History, and we had got to know Miss Muriel Roch, the Head Mistress and some of her staff in the meantime.

Nothing positive developed until a joint conservation force was formed with the boys of Denstone, under the leadership of the biology master there. He brought a mixed party of sixth formers with the object of doing active conservation projects. He wanted them to plant trees or clear scrub or to do other work more calculated, it seemed to me, to benefit their muscles than their minds.

Although it was doubtless a fine way of taking the surplus fizz out of hefty boys, it did not seem so good for girls. But they dug an artificial fox earth in Primrose Dell and built a corrugated steel sheet hide about twenty yards away on the other side of the bank.

Foxes will take to artificial earths almost as freely as tits to a nesting box and the position of this one is ideal. It is about thirty yards from the boundary of Squitch Bank, which rises up in a mountain of plough behind it. The hide is so placed that it overlooks the drainpipe entrances of the earth, with the sun slanting across from the East in the morning and the west at night, with varying angles from behind all day.

It was a worthwhile project because there was at least a chance of reward for the hard labour of construction in opportunities to photograph a litter of cubs through their growing weeks or to watch them at leisure, if the foxes found the place attractive enough to occupy.

Digging in such heavy, cloying clay was mauling work and it was interesting to watch the one or two boys who took pride in their virility flexing their muscles as they heaved out each shovelful of lumpy spoil. The rest were made of management stuff and knew by instinct that the most simple task will stand a foreman, so they contented themselves with proffering advice. The girls were more conscientious and, by and large, their comments shrewder.

Last year the boys didn't turn up, presumably because they had found more profitable furrows to plough, or more scientific, so I was invited once more to the School of St Mary and St Anne.

Discussing the potential here with the senior biology class, I found that Liz Moonie, one of the girls from the year before, had been away on a course to a Field Study Centre, working on methods of trapping and marking and classifying small mammals.

The conventional way of trapping small mammals is with Longworth traps, which are long square boxes, made in sections from aluminium sheet. When a small animal enters, he trips a trigger which shuts the door behind him.

When the biologist comes round he can take out the captive unharmed, weigh and measure him, and mark him by clipping a simple pattern in his fur, fitting an identification tag or clipping the nail off a toe.

There are all sorts of sophisticated experiments to try then, some of which I feel are of more academic than practical value. Complicated mathematical formulae calculate from the frequency the same animals are recaptured what the local population is. The snag is that food and warm bedding have to be placed in the traps and the cleverest animals soon discover this and return for a second helping. So the frequency of recapture is sometimes related to the Intelligence quotient and may be a measure of mousish spivvery as well as of the local population density. This is called 'trap addiction' for the satisfied animals find the traps irresistible as those who are 'hooked' find drugs.

The animals which end up in owl talons instead of returning to schedule may well upset results or vandals may steal the traps. This can be quite a serious expense because traps cost almost £2 each and there are likely to be upwards of twenty set out at five yard intervals over a grid on the territory being studied.

The important thing from my point of view was not the pure research but to devise experiments of sufficient interest to fire the enthusiasm of the next generation.

The welfare of our wildlife so obviously depends more on the interest and goodwill of those to come than on anything the zealots can do today.

I was anxious that the girls should not be expected to cut down trees or dig ditches till their muscles ached and their spirits flagged. It seemed far more sensible for them to do something exciting, if possible, but at least interesting enough for them to want to carry on the work when they left school.

Whatever the anti-sport brigade may say, the instinct to hunt is ingrained in normal folk. I once watched a party of bird watchers catching swans for ringing, while they were flightless during the moult and had retreated to the centre of Blithfield Reservoir for sanctuary.

The ornithologists arrived, studious and serious as choir boys during funeral mass. I would lay odds that each would have added his reverend signature to any petition aimed at preventing other people from coursing or shooting or hunting.

They were rugged up like mountaineers in anoraks and solemnly climbed into a fleet of motor boats. The leaders of each group were armed with long bamboo poles, tipped with metal hooks like shepherds' crooks. These hooks were made the right size to go round a swan's neck and pull him towards the boat, instead of being large enough for sheep.

I am sure that, if it had occurred to them, they would all have regretted any discomfort they might cause the birds, but that they felt virginally innocent because the whole operation was so transparently in the cause of purest science. They simply wanted to catch the swans, place rings upon any whose legs did not already display such adornment and tabulate the particulars of any swans which had been marked before.

This would determine the age of each bird, and probably how far he had come since tangling with the last bird ringers. It might show his marital status and perhaps confirm theories that swans are not averse to wife swapping and are far from the paragons of virtue some would have us believe.

Interesting, no doubt, but I wondered if the swans thought the discomfort involved in being heaved out of the water by a hook round their necks, was repaid by the mass of theories the scientists dreamed up.

The boats set off and the herd of swans was slowly rounded up and inched into the shallow water at one end of the reservoir. Everyone behaved with exemplary decorum.

Then a swan broke through the closing line of boats and flapped off for the safety of the centre of the water. The nearest boat wheeled round and set off in pursuit, to prevent the rest of the birds following in a sheepish dash for freedom.

I never saw men transformed more magically. One second they were desiccated scholars in a dispassionate search for knowledge, the next they were primitive men. As the distance between the boat and the quarry diminished their faces cracked into glints of anticipation which showed through their civilised façade. No pig sticker, spear outstretched at full gallop, was more slave to barbaric emotions than these men who would stoutly deny any zest for hunting in their calmer moments. The skill with which the leader wielded his swan crook was no less than a hunter hot blooded after pig and the thrill of conquest as he heaved the swan unharmed into the well of the boat was as fierce as if he had pitched a pig in the dust.

I see no point in pretending that human nature has suddenly altered or that our civilisation is more than scratch deep. The fact is that the urge to hunt is as basic a human instinct as eating or making love, so that it is sensible not to try to repress it but to channel it into useful ways.

Although they would probably deny it, the swan catchers obviously enjoyed the chase as much as the knowledge their researches uncovered. So whatever the temporary discomfort involved, it was of long term benefit to the birds because nobody bothers about protecting threatened species unless they are deeply interested in their welfare. And the surest way of ensuring a future for our wildlife is to encourage hobbies which would be impossible without it.

I was therefore delighted that Liz Moonie wanted to do some live trapping as a result of the field study course she had attended.

John Thompson, the Regional Officer of the Nature Conservancy chipped in with the loan of twenty traps and half a dozen girls turned up to start the project.

Liz and her friend Lois Millar were leaders, old stagers from the year before, and they were helped by girls a year younger who we hoped would carry on to give continuity the following year.

They chose part of Ley Close, just above the pit of Primrose Dell, which had regenerated into a tangle of undergrowth after the trees were felled there six years ago. They put stakes at five yard intervals and set their traps precisely and exactly according to the theory of the Field Study course.

Next day, Liz came rushing up to the house, flushed and excited as Diana the goddess of hunting herself. She had caught a mouse. *Clethrionomys glareolus britannicus,* the short tailed vole glared truculently at me from inside a plastic bag. If it had been a man eating tiger it could have not been more welcome and, when I had been suitably convinced of the effectiveness of the traps and the skill of the trappers, the small animal was taken back to the spot where it was caught.

A tiny patch of fur was clipped from its shoulder for subsequent identification, then lengths of head and body and legs and tail were measured, and its private parts scrutinised to establish its sex. Then it was set free.

I was as delighted as the girls but for a different reason. I felt that any mental barrier which had been erected years before, when I had prevented access at will to several hundred girls, had been demolished by this mouse. Far more important, this first mouse had so obviously fired their interest that some of them might continue to care enough in future to see that our birthright of wildlife is not swapped for the potage of progress.

Next day and the day after the catch went up to half a dozen or so, including the first one which was recaptured and had another bit of fur snipped off for his timerity.

There must be a very high density of voles and shrews and long tailed field mice in that part of the wood because the girls achieved a very high percentage of success, sometimes making a capture in over half the traps they set.

It was very satisfactory but the elation didn't last long. Although it was only October, we got a sudden cold spell and, when they visited their traps next day, several mice were dead.

The effect of several cold hours in a metal box, even though it was supplied with bedding, had not occurred to the girls but there was absolutely no excuse for me not warning them. I knew perfectly well what might happen but had not taken the trouble to listen to the overnight weather report on the wireless. If I had, I should have sprung the traps.

The impact on the girls was dramatic. They had started the experiment crammed with enthusiasm, avid in search of knowledge, and their initial success had spurred them on.

It had never even crossed their minds that they would harm so much as a hair on the head of their quarry, so that they had subconsciously felt the pure thrill of the chase without its sordid climax. When they discovered that they had unwittingly killed their victims, not because they were pests, as one traps a mouse in the kitchen, but for mere curiosity, they were sickened with trapping. They gathered the Longworth traps up, took them back to clean and polish them, and returned them to their packing case.

I was just as disappointed as they were but, though I felt we were almost back where we had started, I was determined that all should not be lost.

Lois Millar and Sally Holdick had started with a group to see what the effect on vegetation would be when the bottom of Primrose Dell was filled with water.

I had persuaded a man with a mechanical ditching

machine, who had been working locally, to dam the outlet where water draining into the dell spills over into a ditch on the next farm. My idea was to make a pool at the north end of the wood to attract a wide variety of wildlife because the area is so isolated and quiet.

Before it started to fill Lois and her team surveyed it and plotted the ground contours accurately. They took a transect across it on which they made a complete census of all vegetation growing there, and drove in a stake calibrated in feet so that they could record the changing levels of the water.

It will take a year or so to be sure what effect on the surroundings changing the level of the water table has had, but at least it is not likely to trail tragedy in its wake.

Meanwhile Liz Moonie and I are devising other means of studying the small mammal population. She is searching for undigested owl and hawk pellets so that she can examine them for the skulls and bones of their victims because the ratio of different species caught by predators is likely to be proportional to the ratio of live survivors in the area which have so far escaped predation.

We are putting small sheets of corrugated iron flat on the ground and noting what is disturbed from under them when they are lifted and when the weather gets warm again in summer, perhaps the Longworth traps will come out of retirement to confirm the findings of less scientific methods.

Every Saturday night the ride opposite the house through Dunstal Pool Plantation glows with an eerie light. It emanates from a mercury arc lamp in a contraption placed at the intersection of the rides to cast its rays as far as possible.

John Herbert is writing a thesis for his biology teacher training course and the subject he decided to investigate was the moth population of this area.

The wood was once part of the ancient forest of Needwood and there are pretty comprehensive records made by local naturalists for more than fifty years. Most of these records were obtained by sugaring or netting by hand. Sugaring consisted in painting the bark of trees with a solution of sugar or rum-and-sugar and rounding up the drunks next morning.

John Herbert's method is far more scientific. Moths have phototropic eyes. They are highly sensitive to light intensity and each eye is coupled to the muscle network on the opposite side of the body. If the intensity of light is brighter on the insect's right side, its left wing will be stimulated to flap faster, pivoting it towards the light so that it automatically 'homes' on a bright source of light.

The mercury arc lamp is placed in a container covered by a perspex cone, broken up by metal baffles. Moths home on to this cone, collide with the baffles and fall down into the trap.

I put the light on every Saturday night and John Herbert comes next morning to catalogue his catch. When he has recorded it, he places the moths carefully under dense vegetation, where they will not be found by insectiverous birds, so that they escape unharmed next night.

We take great care with this lamp because it could be devastating. It is so ruthlessly efficient that it could literally milk the wood of the very creatures we are trying to encourage. So I only light it once a week and he is conscientious that he puts his captives safe where they will not be as vulnerable as food on a bird table.

During his two year experiment he has caught moths in every month of the year, of a hundred and thirty different species some of which are rare.

He is comparing these to the records of his predecessors, hoping to find some which eluded them but also watching out for species which they found but are absent now. We shall then try to establish the reason for any absentees and, if it is because their food plants no longer flourish here, we shall replant some in an effort to reintroduce any that no longer find this place attractive.

Daffodil Lawn, at the far end of Holly Covert, has long been famous for its wild daffodils. Before we moved in, it was not uncommon to catch perfect strangers digging out the bulbs and the flowers were so raided that they had no chance to seed. A previous tenant is said to have grown so fed-up with the trespass they caused that he broke them up annually with a chain harrow to minimise their charms. When we arrived the blooms were decreasing but, by resisting the temptation to pick them ourselves and discouraging others, the trend has been reversed and they are beginning to spread again. The same meadow is rich in wood anemones, both white and pink, and wild violets, with carpets of bluebells under the trees around the edge. There are cowslips and even I am ashamed of the crop of buttercups, though I do nothing about them lest I put the other flowers at risk.

Primrose Dell is not only rich in primroses but blind wild strawberries and the slope down from the rest of Ley Close is clothed in giant mare's tail which makes it look like a primeval forest.

The area which the Forestry Commission cleared for replanting after the trees were felled is a wonderful sanctuary for a wide variety of birds. All through summer the daylight hours are sibilant with the ventriloquial notes of grasshopper warblers and, when they die down at dusk, the nightjars pick up the song and make the evening air rich with their churring.

There are whinchats and redstarts, all three varieties of woodpecker, tree pipits and tits and warblers in profusion.

Woodcock breed here, and tree creepers and most of the common woodland birds.

There were a lovely lot of curlew when we came but draining the park has destroyed their nesting habitat, though we still hear occasional ones fly over. It is a potential paradise for birds, but although we found them in great variety, their numbers were not very high because of the degree of predation and disturbance.

CHAPTER EIGHT

The reward

Despite the publicity surrounding the 1970 European Conservation Year, there is nothing new about nature conservation, which is as old as gamekeeping.

Having the highest admiration for the effectiveness of good gamekeepers, I decided to manage these woods on their principles, but to concentrate on helping a wide variety of threatened creatures instead of doing good only to pheasants and partridges.

The methods keepers use are really very simple. They endeavour to give their charges such a sense of security, by keeping their beat secluded and undisturbed, that they do not want to wander from it.

They cultivate good breeding habitat and plenty of food, in great variety to limit the temptation to imagine that the grass over the boundary could possibly be greener. They fight battles for the weak by waging war on the predators of game.

I set about the grey squirrels first. The fact that I have accounted for between five and six hundred gives some idea of their previous density. We poked them out of dreys and shot them with twelve bores and rifles, trapped them in tunnel traps and caught them with dogs.

The lurchers are surprisingly clever at this and the squirrels surprisingly stupid. Like all the greyhound breeds, lurchers hunt by sight and have an uncanny knack of spotting a squirrel feeding on the ground or in low bushes at a great distance or in thick cover.

When they see one, they streak away and the squirrel, hearing them coming, seeks safety in height. He shins up the nearest tree and squats, motionless as an ancient knot, in a fork somewhere near the top.

Unless I have got a rifle, which is not often, he would be perfectly safe in the knowledge that the dogs and I would soon grow tired and go away. But squirrels are not famous for their steady nerves. The dogs dance, barking round the base of the tree, like trumpeters round the walls of Jericho and crack the squirrel's nerves. He decides that some other tree, almost any other tree, is safer and runs along the branches to the slenderest twigs before leaping for a hold on the next tree.

The dogs' excitement knows no bounds and they dance in frenzy underneath, each high pitched bark spurring their quarry to a further leap till he misses his foothold and leaps his last.

The number of fledglings and eggs that the squirrels must have destroyed hardly bears thinking about and it seemed surprising that there were any small birds left for them to catch.

I have also killed a lot of rats since we have been here but, unlike keepers, I do no harm to stoats and weasels because I like to see them about, though I might be forced to get tough if their population exploded.

By far the most dramatic lesson I have learned is the value of leaving an area like Dunstal Pool Plantation undisturbed.

Apart from encouraging nearly the whole heronry to concentrate there, the sanctuary has proved irresistible to the fallow deer.

The Forestry Commission control the numbers of deer on the land they either own or rent by employing a game warden to cull any surplus to the number the terrain will sustain in winter. It is obvious that if more deer are allowed to colonise an area smaller than the lowest seasonal food supply will sustain, which is normally in winter, then they will be forced to stray on to adjacent farms and gardens where they will do damage.

The fallow deer spend part of their time here and part in Bagot's Wood, so Gerald Springthorpe, the Commission game warden, assesses the effects the whole herd will have on the whole area.

A rough rule of thumb is that it is necessary to cull about one in six each year to keep the population steady. In other words their natural increase is about 15% per annum. So he calculates the total number he will have to take out, taking into consideration how much they have increased in the season and what complaints there are of damage, and he selects the worst specimens for removal.

In Bagot's Wood he removes the limpers first. The ground is cold wet clay and some of the deer here seem to get a form of septic arthritis, which cripples them if they are left. He takes these first and any with bad heads, and then he adjusts the ratio of the sexes to avoid too many bucks.

The result is that the total herd is kept to the largest size that will not do serious damage on local farms and the quality of the survivors is improved by this selective culling out the bad as surely as livestock breeders improve their herds by selective choice of breeding stock.

The other way he selects his cull is to take out most animals in the area where he gets most complaints from farmers, who would take the law into their own hands otherwise, so that he is able to leave ours almost untouched.

The result is that the deer have discovered that they are not disturbed here and that, provided that they lie up in Dunstal Pool Plantation nobody ever approaches them.

I go round the rides several times a day and take a pot

shot at the crows on winter evenings. The deer have got so used to seeing me and the dogs that they often don't even bother to get up even if they are lying within fifteen yards of the ride.

I decided to do some experiments to see if this could be put to practical use, and I discovered some simple facts. Although they will let me get so close as I walk past, they go at once if I stop. The implication is that they will tolerate regular movement past them but take no risk when once it appears that they are the subjects of attention.

In walking past them, it is vital to avoid getting between them and their natural line of retreat, for the instant they suspect that they might find themselves surrounded they flee in panic.

One old black doe, who is the matriarch of our winter herd and had twins two years ago, is now so sure of herself that she stamps her foot at me, as an angry ewe would do and follows me down the wood as if she would really see me off. But if I call her bluff by moving into a dangerous or even unusual position, she won't return for a couple of days.

It is a lesson which might be useful to public authorities who administer land where deer are regarded as a valuable amenity for the public to enjoy.

On Cannock Chase, in our area, about sixty deer are killed every year by motor cars, mostly at rush hours or pub closing times, particularly at weekends.

So many people, often with unruly dogs, go on the Chase at that time that the deer take refuge in adjacent woodland and are knocked down by cars when they return. If the authorities could only control where the public wander, leaving secluded areas where wildlife was not only left in peace but had such security that they believed disturbance impossible, the deer and birds would grow tamer and the public would find that a little discipline had helped them to enjoy the natural amenities much more.

When I have gone round the pool plantation, the deer there know that I will have scattered maize and barley in the ride opposite the house. Almost before my footsteps have died away, they come out to feed in full view of my study and the sitting-room windows so that we can enjoy their grace and beauty as we relax.

I often see a fox, which also lies up there, and wild badgers and birds of all sorts are usually about.

Since describing my experiments with hand-reared badgers in detail in *Badgers At My Window,* I have been forced to keep them within a six and a half acre enclosure with the roe deer instead of allowing them to wander where they liked outside the fence.

This has been entirely for their own protection because the sister of my hand-reared sow was hanged in a snare and there was obvious danger that my old tame Bill Brock and his mate would suffer the same fate, for I obviously have no control over what is done over my boundary nor what danger my badgers court when they are away. So I was forced to bolt up their badger gate out into the wood and had to put twenty-seven tons of concrete round the base of the fence to discourage them from digging out.

The enclosure they are in contains a wide variety of terrain including the paddock in front of the house, Dunstal Pool and the marsh around it, two stands of mixed woodland, a newly planted spinney and thick patches of bracken and rushes where the roe deer have their kids.

It was naturally disappointing to have to coop them in an enclosure when I had so wanted to give them complete freedom and to uncover facts about their territorial behaviour in return.

But although they have only six acres instead of the wide world as their playground, it does not seem to inconvenience them very much as they rarely bother to dig out and soon return if they do, and I am convinced that it was wise to constrain them.

When the little sow was killed there were a great many wild badgers in the wood. We often saw them on summer evenings and they wore strong 'runs' or paths round the edge of the netting where they walked round the boundary of our badgers' territory, presumably uttering threats to each other in passing.

Now there isn't a run at all outside our fence and we rarely see a wild badger because they have deserted some of the traditional setts they have occupied for generations. I do not know if they have been snared or gassed or poisoned or trapped, but there is no doubt in my mind that some human hand is guilty.

Although my badgers cannot enjoy their full freedom, the extent of their territory is sufficient to allow them to lead reasonably full lives. They have the choice of two artificial setts, the one under an old hawthorn tree within twenty yards of the sitting-room window and the other down by Dunstal Pool. Each consists of a heavy plank kennel, let in level with the surface of the ground, with a hinged lid for inspection. The badgers enter and leave at will through a subterranean tunnel of nine inch drain pipes made of unglazed earthenware.

The original bedding was straw but they scratched it out and replaced it with reeds and grass and bracken, which they change as the spirit moves them.

A pivoted lever protrudes into the tunnel entrance of each sett so that the badgers have to push it aside whenever they leave or return and, as it pivots, it triggers off a micro-switch wired to a barograph in my study.

This is fitted with an electromagnet which marks the moving roll of graph paper each time the lever in the tunnel is deflected. As a result I have been able to compile an accurate record of every emergence and re-entry the badgers have made from either sett for more than the last two years. I know at precisely what time they came out for the first time in the evening, when they returned in the morning and how often they went back to the sett during the night.

This has provided original knowledge which would have been impossible to obtain visually during the hours of darkness, quite apart from the thousands of hours that would have been spent fruitlessly when nothing was happening.

I used to imagine from watching wild badgers in the field that they came out at dusk, went off to forage all night, and returned at dawn. Now I know that they often return many times in the interval, for my graphs show far more activity around the sett than I ever suspected.

Two bulbs near the television are wired to the main circuit in the barograph so that I have warning of impending activity before the badgers emerge. When one of these bulbs lights up, I stop watching the little box and look out of the window to 'live' entertainment, illuminated by a floodlight near the sett. This not only makes observation easy and comfortable, but it obviates unproductive waste of time.

I have described this in more detail in *Badgers At My Window*, but since then I have added one refinement. John Burton, of the B.B.C. Natural History Unit, loaned equipment and helped me to 'bug' the sett for sound. We fitted a microphone inside the kennel of the sett and wired it to a loud speaker in my study. It is so sensitive that it amplifies the sound of the badgers breathing so that, when I switch on each morning, I can tell if one or both animals have returned simply by counting their respirations.

The only technical snag was that the microphone is so sensitive that it picked up the almost incessant background hum of aircraft noise which pollutes our atmosphere, but a large pile of straw bales, heaped over the sett effectively blanketed most of that din out. The badgers must have been almost as pleased as I was.

I often leave the speaker switched on while I am sitting at my study desk. I normally detest houses which have the background noise of music because my powers of concentration are such that I need quiet to think. But the somnolent snores and grunts and stertorous breathing of badgers is a comfortable and relaxing sound. They sleep the deep sleep of those with easy consciences.

When I turn the speaker on at breakfast, their respiration rate is slow and deep as they sleep off the effects of the food and exercise of their hard night's work. But about an hour before they emerge in the evening, there is a clatter as loud as castinets. This is made by their incisor teeth clacking together as they groom and shine their fur.

Sometimes when Bill Brock, the old boar, has come in the house and been lying in my lap in deep contentment, he has nibbled the hair on the back of my hand and on my wrist, making the same 'castinet' sounds as he does so.

It is obviously a display of affection, but badgers are rough lovers and, underrating his own prodigious strength, he sometimes includes a painful tweak in his repertoire of love.

I imagine he does the same thing to the little sow in the sett, for the rhythmic clatter of his teeth is sometimes punctuated by sharp squeaks and squeals. The badgers' equivalent, I dare say, of 'Go easy, my lover, you're pinching!'

I believe this mutual grooming may have been underrated as a technique for limiting aggression among wild badgers. Naturalists have often noticed that, although there may be several adult boars in a colony, they do not appear to fight.

The usual explanation is that the frequency with which

they 'spot' each other with musk from their anal glands must give them all a 'colony scent' which prevents them from fighting animals with the same smell as themselves.

I wonder if mutual grooming serves the same purpose? It would be difficult to devise a more efficient technique for acquiring the same body scent as one's companion than nibbling her gently from head to foot and encouraging her to reciprocate.

Perhaps the most exciting sound to fill my study was on an evening in April 1970. I turned the speaker on to see if there were any signs of imminent emergence and heard an extraordinary guttural chattering. Badgers have an affection call, not unlike a quiet stallion's whinney, but the notes of this were higher pitched and obviously more urgent. There was also an occasional deep growl.

I have kept ferrets all my life and they are very vocal when mating, for the jill resists the male's advances, sometimes for hours. All the mustilidae seem to be lusty lovers, as our forefathers noticed when they coined the phrase 'a bit of a stoat' for an over-enthusiastic man.

The sound the badgers were making reminded me of this except that the sow's protests seemed more for effect than from her heart, and the boar's confident persistence suggested that he was taking her 'No' to mean no more than 'Maybe'.

I removed the lead from the loud speaker and plugged it into the tape recorder to freeze the conversation for posterity.

Their vocal display continued with such clarity that any sleazy private-eye could have translated it into evidence strong enough to stand up in any court of law.

I seem to have plugged in at the beginning of the dialogue which continued at increasing pace as the love-making hotted-up. The sounds were so clear that the changing rate of the boar's respirations told the whole tale till silence reigned again. Then he shook himself, ruffed up the straw and left the sett to feed. The little sow went back to sleep.

It was satisfying to be, so far as I know, the first man to record the sounds of such a mating, especially as the normal rut is supposed to take place between July and November. Though circumstantial, this was the first evidence that badgers may mate in spring.

I was able to add visual weight to the evidence when the sow allowed me to handle her two days later and it was obvious from her distended vulva that she was still on heat. Two separate boars went into the cage trap I keep set in the perimeter fence at about the same time, one the night before and the other the night after. I was able to prove that they were different boars because I marked them with sheep dye of different colours before I let them go again.

Badgers have an unusual physiological quality called 'delayed implantation'. The embryo, formed after fertilisation does not immediately become implanted on the wall of the uterus, and the embryo does not develop further until it does.

The delay of implantation varies, though the rut of badgers is generally supposed to be between July and November but the tiny embryo seems to be implanted on the uterus wall at about the same time of year, irrespective of when the mating took place. The result is that all young badgers seems to be born in early spring.

If the mating of my badgers in April proves to be successful, it will mean that the tiny embryo remained free in the uterus for up to eight months before the implantation took place to allow the foetus to develop.

There can be quite a kick from discovering even such a tiny fragment of original knowledge, however insignificant its commercial potential may be, so that I am thankful that

I no longer have to measure time in terms of cash.

One of our female roe deer produced a kid in four years out of five. All the roe also live within the perimeter fence, so I was very pleased because they are generally considered difficult in captivity or even under our type of controlled conditions. It was a yardstick of the fact that they are contented with their lot.

The chief difficulty we found in rearing them before has been their susceptibility to internal parasites, but by deliberately keeping the ground understocked and by worming regularly, the young have done quite well.

I wondered this year what would happen now that the badgers were also fastened in and could no longer go as far as they liked to forage and fritter away their energies. I know that badgers kill rabbits when they get the chance and a new born roe kid is no bigger. The doe leaves it alone in a form as a hare leaves her leverets, and she only goes at intervals to suckle it.

In previous years it had been five or six weeks before the roe kids had been considered strong enough by their mothers to be allowed to accompany them while they were grazing. Till then, motionless concealment had been deemed wiser than seeking safety in flight.

I wasn't afraid the badgers would hunt them out deliberately, as a fox might have done, but I was worried lest a badger bumbled on them accidentally.

One night I happened to notice the roe doe go to a thick patch of reeds near the sett where the boar badger was sleeping, suckle her kid and leave it within twenty yards of danger.

I waited an hour or so, till the bulb on the television warned that the badger was on his way out, and I prepared, if necessary, to rush to the rescue.

He scratched, used his latrine pit and wandered off in the general direction of the form where the kid was lying.

He certainly wasn't hunting it deliberately, but just grubbing about in the grass for slugs and beetles, approaching nearer the kid by pure blind chance.

I do not know where the doe was lying, for she had vanished as soon as she had fed and groomed her kid. But when the badger crossed some imaginary danger line she appeared as if by magic. She came at him like a bull, not charging head down, but coming like a racehorse for the finishing post. She kicked down as she went over him, turned twenty yards away and attacked again from a fresh angle.

The poor old badger had been mooching along, minding his own business and plotting harm to no one. He simply didn't know what had hit him, and while he was pondering, it hit him again. So he turned for home at full speed, with the doe flushed with victory following up her advantage, and buffeting him several times more on the way.

My barograph showed that he didn't venture out again for two hours and a half. It was another example of the advantages of living on the spot, with time to burn and the added aid of mechanical devices to prompt the moment when it will be profitable to settle down to watch. Under such circumstances it may be as profitable simply to sit, with an open mind, as it is to sit and think.

The reason why helpless roe kids can survive, even in areas where such omniverous feeders as badgers abound, may be unimportant in terms of material prosperity, but I found the spectacle rewarding beyond price.

It reminded me that, when I came to Goat Lodge, I was an escapist, yearning to get away from the stresses of modernity. I wanted peace and relaxation and the chance to avoid people with whom I had nothing in common. I wanted to shed off a few centuries so that I could share my wilderness with wild creatures whose ancestors were here before mine were claiming to be civilised.

It has proved to be a modest aspiration. Reality has proved so far superior to the dream. I found at first that the luxury of enjoying pleasures which had only been pipe dreams before was more than enough. It was exciting when specialist naturalist friends discovered rarities unrecognised by me.

A botanist found what he believed to be the first wild servis tree recorded in these parts and John Herbert trapped moths almost as rare. Wild flowers and bird songs are a joy here in spring and it is thrilling to watch at arm's length how the fallow bucks mark out their rutting stands in October and defend their does till they are spent and the younger bucks usurp them.

These are passive joys. The first experiment with the herons drove home what possibilities lay in a positive policy of wildlife management. There are only five heronries in the whole county of Staffordshire and 'our' heronry has increased from insignificance to the largest in the county.

I had proved that, by creating a sense of security in Holly Covert, by controlling predators and staying out myself, the number of creatures it harboured literally rocketed.

I believe that the greatest danger for our wildlife in the future is that it will be ousted from its shrinking number of congenial refuges by the sheer pressure of humanity; that we are in real peril of killing the very things we love.

Working hours are shrinking too and transport is so much easier that a nostalgic interest in everything rural deepens as life in crowded towns grows ever more artificial.

There are now so many divergent interests competing for the countryside that there is real danger that it will lose its greatest charm of undisturbed seclusion.

So I have decided to make this a real sanctuary and to be equally ruthless with curious visitors, and predators and trespassers. I improve the habitat by planting berried shrubs and brambles and hazel nuts and other forms of nourishment and nesting cover. It worries me no more that foresters think I give aid to weeds than that would-be visitors deem me inhospitable.

I get bored with holidays and, finding nowhere I prefer to home, I do not go abroad. I spend my money instead on some improvement which I hope will still be giving me pleasure when bikini clad girls on a holiday beach have long since grown fat and gross.

One year I hired a bulldozer to enlarge Dunstal Pool to leave an island for nesting duck and as a roosting refuge the badgers wouldn't disturb. The spoil was pushed into a heap which I sowed with grass and in which I dug an artificial badger sett I could see from the window.

When we came, we had a wire netting fence to keep roe deer out of the garden, but my wife thought it looked like a concentration camp. So the bulldozer came again, this time to dig out a dry moat, to make a Ha-ha so that our view was unobstructed. There is another badger sett, within twenty yards of the sitting-room window, constructed from the spoil of that year's holiday.

The young hedge along the drive is six hundred yards long, of mixed hawthorn and blackthorn. When that grows and thickens, it should contain a delightful variety of birds' nests in spring and provide berries and sloes for the pheasants in winter. There will still be enough sloes left over to make a bottle of sloe gin liqueur for us at Christmastide.

Sooner or later the Corsican pines planted by the Forestry Commission will grow up till their canopy crowds out the nesting cover which is ideal at the moment for nightjars and grasshopper warblers.

Luckily (for us!) there is enough honey fungus to kill off quite large patches of these trees, so that *all* the nesting cover may not be obliterated. The Commission are most co-operative and I hope to cut one more major radial ride through Lord's Coppice and another through Cockshutt Close to Primrose Dell.

The ride through Dunstal Pool Plantation looks tall as a cathedral nave as I lie in bed at dawn on misty mornings, and if only two other rides converged to the same point, they would be superb for observation.

It would then be possible to see a fox or a deer cross one ride and, by waiting quietly to plot his progress wherever he went in the wood, perhaps uncovering odd snippets of knowledge which hadn't come to light before.

There is always a thrill from such discoveries, but I get less delight from a thirst for knowledge than from far simpler pleasures.

When Tough, my alsatian died, I replaced her with Tick, a German short haired pointer bitch. An odd choice for a naturalist, you may think, but I never had a better dog.

She has a more hospitable nature than either Tough or I because she is delighted to see almost anyone who calls. But generations of selective breeding for sport have made her physically strong and mentally bright and biddable. She is the perfect companion for a country walk because her delicate nose tells her of the presence of all sorts of creatures which would have lain hidden and undiscovered without her. She wanders ten or fifteen yards ahead and freezes statuesque 'pointing' at some insignificant bush or clump of cover.

That is all she does unless I tell her to flush her quarry. Otherwise she doesn't disturb it but waits quietly while I investigate or call her on to leave it undisturbed as I see fit.

When we return home from such a walk, I can amuse

myself for hours sitting by the window, watching the visitors to the bird table.

It is simply an old grindstone from a cornmill, mounted on three rick straddles and I bait it with corn and flaked maize and apples and cheese and fat. The roe deer come up for the flaked maize and barley and a flock of collared doves, sometimes nearly a hundred strong gorge on anything they fancy. We get woodpeckers and tits for the fat and the tame ptarmigan pigeons and humble robins and blackbirds and tree sparrows and house sparrows. There is continuous movement of changing colours and always the chance of a surprise rarity.

It isn't often that such a pleasant life gets recognition but the Nature Conservancy, sharing my concern for threatened species, have helped my work here by scheduling the land as a Site of Special Scientific Interest.

In practice this means that any planning application for change of land usage would be brought automatically to the notice of the Conservancy who would be likely to back the experiments I am doing and see that planning authorities took them seriously. This was also recognised by the Countryside Commission who marked European Conservation Year by giving a hundred Countryside 1970 awards to those 'who had produced physical improvement to the countryside or contributed to the increasing awareness and understanding of the countryside'. The awards were presented by Prince Philip, mostly to organisations with rural interests, and I was one of the handful of lucky private individuals to receive one.

I believe that it is possible to produce an artificially high density of wildlife, as gamekeepers have done for generations. All that is necessary is to choose a varied terrain, which may have no great commercial or amenity value, and manage it for the benefit of threatened species instead of game. Instead of being shot for sport, the surplus will then spill over into the surrounding countryside, where it can thrive and be enjoyed by the public as an amenity.

Such places could be links in a chain of reserves, kept secluded and managed to make good the losses caused by human pressures.

It is satisfying and creative work and, if my experiments are successful, perhaps one day my beloved wilderness will be a pilot for others which may succeed in preserving a heritage for the future.

Index

Index